Alastair Mars first went to sea in 1932 and at an early age joined submarines, with which he remained until the end of the war with Japan. After his year commanding *Unbroken* he was appointed Assistant Staff Officer (Operations) to the Flag Officer Commanding Submarines, in London, and helped plan the midget submarine attack on *Tirpitz*. The following year he returned to active service in command of the submarine *Thule* in the Far East. For his work in extensive combined operations of a very special nature he was awarded a bar to his D.S.C. In all he completed, during his war service, thirty war patrols of an average duration of three weeks; he was heavily depth-charged on fifteen occasions, reported sunk five times, and survived many air and gun attacks.

Also by Alastair Mars
SUBMARINES AT WAR 1930-1945
and published by Corgi Books

Alistair Mars
D.S.O., D.S.C. and Bar

UNBROKEN

The Story of a Submarine

CORGI BOOKS
A DIVISION OF TRANSWORLD PUBLISHERS LTD

UNBROKEN

A CORGI BOOK 0 552 09900 7

Originally published in Great Britain
by Frederick Muller Ltd.

PRINTING HISTORY
Frederick Muller edition published 1953
Frederick Muller edition reprinted nine times
Corgi edition published 1975

This low-priced Corgi Book has been completely reset in a
type face designed for easy reading, and was printed from
new plates. It contains the complete text of the
original hard-cover edition.

Corgi Books are published by Transworld Publishers Ltd.,
Cavendish House, 57–59 Uxbridge Road,
Ealing, London, W.5.
Made and printed in Great Britain by
Hunt Barnard Printing Ltd., Aylesbury, Bucks.

To the undying memory of

LIEUTENANT JOHN RENWICK
HAIG HADDOW
D.S.C., ROYAL NAVY

and all those Sub-mariners who did
not return

PROLOGUE

A Ship is Born

NOVEMBER, 1941. Kharkov had fallen and the German army advanced through the snows towards Moscow. In Africa the New Zealanders captured Bardia and General Auchinleck launched the offensive that was to result in the relief of Tobruk. In the Mediterranean, the disasters of Greece and Crete still fresh in our minds, we were doing no more than hold our own. The *Ark Royal* had been sunk, and Mr Churchill told Parliament that we were losing a monthly average of 180,000 tons of merchant shipping. While Chiang Kai-shek called upon the Western Powers to join in the war against Japan, America remained uneasily neutral. In Yugoslavia the Chetniks under Mihailovitch harried the German occupation forces. Nuremberg had been bombed and Marshal Pétain led the government of occupied France. The conquest of Abyssinia and the defence of Malta were two bright stars in a black, uncertain night.

At home the people of Britain went about their business with that quiet confidence other nations call arrogance. There was rationing, the Windmill Theatre and jokes about Woolton Pie and the Home Guard . . . Nightly raids on Merseyside and London . . . Walt Disney's 'Fantasia' and the Polish Army choir . . . A million women employed in munitions factories . . . As they hammered rivets, forged steel, and dug at bomb débris, sports fans discussed the recent soccer international in which England had beaten Scotland by two goals to nil. . . .

Farmers tended their fields, fishermen cast their trawls, miners sweated in the ugly darkness of the pits. Aircraft, tanks, bombs and shells rolled from the production lines. Housewives worked miracles with the rations – and found time to drive ambulances and man Wardens' Posts. Children were educated and grandparents came from retirement to 'do their bit'. Parks became allotments, taxis hauled fire pumps. As scientists evolved new and more terrible weapons of destruction, a lunatic fringe demanded 'peace at any price'. In the drive for scrap, park railings became Bren-carriers, dustbins destroyers and aluminium saucepans Spitfires.

And at Barrow-in-Furness in this gloomy, mournful November, as just one tiny part of the great wartime scene, a ship was being born. . . .

It was a grey, depressing afternoon, and as the taxi rattled from the station to the Victoria Park Hotel, my wife huddled closer to my side. Occasionally she shivered, not from cold, but at the bleak melancholy of Barrow. For my part, I was too excited to be affected by the ugliness of industrial Lancashire. At last, after months of nail-biting impatience as captain of a training submarine, I was on my way to take command of the *Unbroken*. She had been launched some months earlier by the wife of 'Tubby' Linton, one of the greatest of all submarine commanders, and was near completion. Only God and the Sea Lords knew what the future held for me, but it could be no worse than the soul-destroying repetition of training duties. Understandably, Ting, my wife, did not see things that way; apart from other considerations, no woman likes to have her husband leave her when she is expecting a baby.

I was twenty-six years old and bubbling with enthusiasm. To use the expression of the day, I was 'mad keen'. Perhaps a little apprehensive, too. For it was no small responsibility

8

to have the lives of thirty-two officers and men dependent, to a very large degree, upon the efficiency of my leadership. In a submarine, fifty fathoms deep, there is no second chance, no opportunity for apologies. With the crew as the fingers, and the captain as the brain, you can compare it to an engineer removing the fuse from an unexploded bomb. When the fingers are supple and responsive the fuse will be removed safely – if the brain transmits the right messages.

It was then my turn to shiver, but with the self-assurance of youth I quickly brushed aside such thoughts and speculated, instead, on how soon I would take the *Unbroken* to sea.

At the hotel we quickly checked our bags and made for the bar. We were greeted by a host of old friends. There was Tubby Linton, waiting to take the submarine *Turbulent* to the Mediterranean; Paul Skelton, standing by to deliver a newly built submarine to the Turks; Lieut.-Commander Maitland-Makgill-Crichton (oddly, he did not boast a nickname, and was always called Maitland-Makgill-Crichton) then captain of the destroyer *Ithurial*. There were others, too, but seeing Paul Skelton affected me most.

The son of a Bishop of Lincoln, he had entered Dartmouth at the same time as myself, and throughout our parallel careers we had remained close friends. Slim, dark, athletic, he filled exactly the popular conception of a naval officer. We had enjoyed and suffered much together. Together we took our sub-lieutenant's course, played games, joined the submarine service, were on the China station, and survived the hideous slaughter of our Mediterranean submarines in the early days of the war. It is a curious thing, but serving in submarines – whether as officer or rating – is like being a member of a Service within a Service. Its members are bound together with a camaraderie unequalled elsewhere, and to me Paul Skelton represents all that is finest in that select body of men.

We have all our own particular memory of the September afternoon when Mr Chamberlain announced the declaration of war. On that Sunday I was navigator of the submarine *Regulus*, and was drinking with a group of friends at the United Services Club, Hong Kong. Apologetically, a Chinese steward told me I was wanted on the telephone. It was Signalman Cheale calling from the *Regulus*. 'Sorry to bother you, sir,' he began, 'but the balloon's gone up. . . .'

I returned to my table, ordered another round of drinks, and broke the news.

A few exclamations, then a long pause. Although there was little we could say, there was another, deeper reason for our silence. We were thinking of the other sub-mariners throughout the Navy, each known to the other, each a friend. Already the boats at home would be patrolling the shallow familiar waters of the North Sea and the Channel. . . .

Exactly six years later, the war over, I sipped a whisky and soda in the ward-room of the submarine *Tudor* as she sailed home from the Far East. Sam Porter, her captain, was one of the few who, like myself, had been sub-mariner before the war. Inevitably, perhaps, we started to work out, with the aid of the Navy List, those who were left. The result was depressingly sad.

Only one in ten remained in the submarine Service. A few had reached the age limit for submarines; strain and sickness had claimed their share. But the majority were dead. We had lost a lot of friends.

And among the dead were included Tubby Linton, V.C., D.S.O., D.S.C., and Paul Skelton. . . .

Of the three submarine commanders knocking back doubles in the bar of the Victoria Park Hotel, I was to be the lucky one. On that November evening in 1941, however, we knew better than to talk of the future. Instead we hid ourselves in the security of the past, and laughed and cracked jokes and raised our glasses. It was not until the early hours that I floated happily to my bed.

*

Vickers' yard at Barrow is a private city of noise and steel; a fevered fantasy in a surrealist nightmare. On the vast slipways the grinning near-skeletons of every type of war vessel, from 8,000-ton cruisers to pathetic, rat-like submarines. Around them, curiously menacing, giant cranes, derricks and monstrous sheer-legs. Then, dwarfing even the cranes, the heavy and light machine shops, the gun-mounting, electrical and battery shops. Armaments stores, engineers' stores, lay-apart stores. Rigging lofts and mould lofts. Greatest of all, the vital, living womb of the shipyard – the gigantic foundries in which heat and metal are fused to mould every limb of every ship to which the yard gives birth. And, above everything, permeating everything, the noise: the screams, groans, howls and agonies of labour. The crashing of steel, the peculiar booming sigh of furnaces, the discordant rattle of cranes and derricks, the harsh clangour of moving parts – a deafening cacophony. Worst of all, the insane, vibrating chatter of riveting that threatens to shake your head from your neck.

With Paul Skelton at my side, I picked my way along the uneven roads of the shipyard to the *Unbroken*, known for signal purposes as P.42. I looked at her – and gasped. Speckled with rust, she was far from completion. The conning-tower and its surrounding structures were in place, but no gun had been fitted, the deck casing was only half completed, there were no periscopes, and a huge rectangular hole in the pressure hull revealed the absence of the motors. Instead of looking a sleek, new submarine, she made me think of a sorely battered hulk salvaged from the ocean depths. Only the barnacles and seaweed were missing.

I turned to Paul Skelton and shouted above the noise: 'I suppose I'm responsible for keeping this sieve afloat.'

He laughed, cupped his hands and bellowed in my ear: 'Lord, no. The firm looks after all that. You don't accept any responsibility until you take her to sea.' He broke off as a short, sour-faced man in overalls passed by. 'Hey, Jock!' he yelled.

The man in overalls walked over. He looked at me speculatively, and with the experience of years, roared effortlessly above the din: 'Och, I know. You dinna have to tell me.' He jerked a thumb as dark and as hard as teak against my chest. 'This gentleman's belonging to yon submarine, an' he's worried.'

I grinned and nodded. The Scot spat expertly into the mud. 'We've been bringing submarines into the worrld for the past forty years. Dinna fret yourself.'

I looked at him with respect, realising, as though for the first time, that the shipyard was made up of more than just steel and noise. Every ship that left Barrow took a part of Jock with her, whether in the sound security of a rivet, the strength of a steel plate, or in the expert adjustment of an electrical lead. His uniform was his dungarees, his medals the scars and callouses on his hands. Tell him so and he would laugh in your face, yet in his heart was the secret pride and knowledge that there would be no battle honours or naval victories without him and his mates in blitz-threatened Barrow.

Meekly I followed Paul Skelton to the office block, feeling strangely confident that order would emerge from the chaos, and that it would not be long before the gloom of November gave way to a sunny, victorious Spring.

I sent the Admiralty a signal to the effect that I had assumed command of the P.42, and on the following day drafted a further signal inquiring about the arrival of my crew. By return I received a detailed message giving me the names and times of arrival of the key members. Names on a sheet of paper. Only one meant anything to me: Sub-Lieutenant John Haddow, who had served with me aboard my training submarine H.44. It was comforting to know he was joining the *Unbroken*, for while the others were as yet no more than ciphers, Haddow was a good, proven officer on whom I knew I could rely.

At last the officers and men of my crew arrived, and when they had been given their billets ashore life became serious.

The *Unbroken* was no longer *my* ship, but *our* ship, and since success and survival depended so greatly upon the efficient running of the boat, and since every man-Jack of us would be responsible for some part of that efficiency, we checked, and re-checked and counter-checked every rivet and split-pin from the top of the periscopes to the base of the keel. Without interfering more than we could help with the work-men engaged on the job – for whom I now had a healthy respect, and who I realised knew more about the mechanics of submarine construction than I was ever likely to know – we watched zealously as the machinery was installed, the engines and torpedo-tubes tested, the 3-inch gun settled on its mounting.

The crew of the *Unbroken* were still no more than names and strange faces to me. I did not worry. At the moment I was interested in them only as seamen and technicians. I knew that once we were afloat I would come to know them well enough as individual personalities, for there is not even the pretence of privacy in the shoulder-rubbing, breath-down-the-neck confines of a submarine. Within a very short space of time everyone, from the Captain to the most junior Ordinary Seaman, would know everyone else's habits, idiosyncrasies, loves, hates, birthmarks, town of origin, pre-war job, favourite swear word, political and religious beliefs, sex life and innermost thoughts. Rhapsodise, if you like, on what a happy band of brothers this made us – and to a degree you would be right – but I knew the inevitable time would come when a man's prayer to God would be in effect: *Please let me be alone for just five minutes, and then let me see a change of face.*

The one facet of their personalities I would have liked to have known at the time I could not know – how, tempera-mentally, they would stand up to a heavy enemy attack. If it came to that, of course, *they* did not know how *I* would stand up to it. In point of fact, neither did I.

*

13

December – the month of Pearl Harbour. The American Navy suffered a vicious, crippling blow, and the events that followed brought blackness to the grey clouds hanging over the civilised world. The Japs invaded Malaya. The *Repulse* and *Prince of Wales* were sunk. Hong Kong fell, Burma was threatened, and half of Malaya was in enemy hands. To help balance these disasters we pushed Rommel from Benghazi, while the Russians held the Germans at the gates of Moscow and Leningrad. The *Gneisenau* and *Scharnhorst* were damaged by the R.A.F., and our submarines penetrated the Arctic to sink thirteen merchantmen. Commandos raided the Lofotens.

Meanwhile, the *Unbroken* neared completion. The periscopes were lowered into position, the motors fitted. In floating dock the rusty hull was burnished and coated with preservative. The vitally important Asdic set was fitted. (Asdic sets are carried by both surface vessels and submarines. In, for example, destroyers, they reveal, by sending out supersonic waves and measuring the echo, the presence, proximity, course and speed of underwater craft. In submarines they serve the same purpose and also work in reverse – they can reveal the presence, speed, etcetera, of surface craft.) The Asdic set installed and tested, a thousand petty details had to be settled, from the fitting of floorboards to the ordering of tablecloths and toilet paper. Our 'teeth' were fitted: eight torpedoes, sleek and blue, each with a warhead containing 1,000 lb. of explosive. Later, supplies came aboard, including a consignment of cabbage which was promptly sent back ashore. The smell of boiling cabbage is bad enough in a kitchen. In a submarine it is even worse – you can't open the windows to get rid of the stink. At last we were able to call in the cleaners who cleared away the mess left by the workmen and made us look more of a slick new fighting ship.

A task I did not relish was giving a pep-talk to the ship's company. I knew what I wanted to say, and my words were sincere enough, but in wartime, when speech-making is a disease, and everyone utters the same exhortations, promises and sentiments as the man before, sincerity is reduced to trite clichés and worn-out platitudes. To say something new you needed to be a Winston Churchill. None the less, a pep-talk was expected of me, and I mustered the ship's company in the office block, and addressed them something like this:

'I shall be an exacting captain. I know what I want down to the smallest detail, and I'm going to get it. You can promise your wives and families that you will return to Britain the crew of a successful submarine.' (This was no small promise at a time when half our submarines entering the Mediterranean were being sunk.) 'I have, however, another, more important duty – to destroy the enemy where-ever he may be found. And we shan't shirk the job of finding him. Therefore we have two jobs – to be successful and to survive. To achieve these I need every ounce of loyalty and strength you can give. Remember that I am the sole arbiter of what is good for you, and my orders are to be obeyed im-plicitly. You may expect work, work, and more work. If any of you joined submarines to get away from discipline you are in for shocks. You will learn more discipline with me than you dreamed of – the proper sort of discipline: self-discipline.

'I don't give a damn what you do ashore, so long as you are ready for your duties at the appointed time. This doesn't mean you can run foul of the shore authorities, and when you do, don't forget that *I* shall have to punish your mis-behaviour. Your officers are young, but they have the weight of my experience and training behind them. Obey them without question, for even a bad order well executed leads to a better result than a good order ruined by indeci-sion. A bad order can be countermanded, a slackly obeyed order leads to confusion. In a submarine confusion means disaster.

'One final thing. What was good enough in other sub-marines will not be good enough here. Nothing is "good enough" for me. I'm going to have the best, and only the best – and you're going to give it to me.'

I dismissed them, hoping I hadn't sounded too pompous. All in all, I think it went down quite well, although later, when walking through the ship, I noticed that in every mess had been pinned up copies of a newspaper advertisement for Mars Bars. It said, as I remember: 'Nothing but the best is good enough for Mars.'

The war did not stop for Christmas, but the ship's company were able to take time off from their work of testing and checking to organise a small dance. Ting and I went along, and we enjoyed a jolly, carefree evening, despite the threat of tomorrow. A few of the ratings' wives had come to Barrow for a last good-bye, and there were moments when I was acutely aware of their speculative and curious glances. The thought troubling them was obvious: What sort of a man is this Lieutenant Mars to whom I must entrust my husband's life? So as I moved among them, joking and laughing, I tried to comfort and reassure – to spread a confidence I was far from feeling deep down in my own heart. The dancing produced a galaxy of local charm, all anxious to console Jack for the hard days to come. I think they achieved their object, for many of the men seemed genuinely sad to leave their consolations when the time came.

On New Year's Eve the officers had a party at the Victoria Park Hotel, and apart from a thick head the morning after, my chief memory of the occasion is of a nautical variation of the dance 'Strip the Willow', the main object of which appeared to be to parade in varying degrees of undress. The chimes of midnight also ushered in my twenty-seventh birthday, and the festivities continued until the early hours with a savage 'last fling' determination.

On a grey, snow-flecked morning, the *Unbroken* was wound out across the dockyard basin for a final test. For the first time, the ship's company went to diving stations – the equivalent of action stations in a surface ship. As 'passengers' we carried dockyard and Admiralty officials and observers.

All hatches except those in the conning-tower were shut and clipped, and I stood alone on the bridge, excited, exhilarated and very proud. No nervousness now. A mere six hundred tons we might be, and our armament no more than a 3-inch gun and four torpedo-tubes, but I felt, with reckless self-assurance, that we were more than a match for the Italian, German and Japanese navies combined!

I leaned over the voice-pipe. 'Open One and Six main vents.'

As the vents were opened, the air in numbers One and Six main ballast tanks was replaced by an inrushing flood of water, and we settled a little in the basin. I ordered the other main vents to be opened until we rode on just the air contained in number Four tank. I shut the voice-pipe cock on the bridge, stepped backwards down the ladder inside the conning-tower, pulled the upper hatch down above my head, pushed home the clips and inserted the locking pins. I slid down the ladder into the control-room and the signalman secured the lower conning-tower hatch after me. 'Up for'ard periscope.' With a hiss it slid from its well.

'All right, Number One?'

'Yes, sir', replied Taylor, the first lieutenant.

I lowered the handles at the side of the periscope and gazed at the surrounding dockyard. 'Open number Four main vent.'

Engine-Room Artificer Lewis flicked a lever. The air rushed from number Four tank. Slowly we sank beneath the level of the water in the basin. As the needles on the depth gauges crept past ten feet I ordered: 'Shut Four main vent.'

The vent of number Four tank was shut, and the air still trapped inside it provided a cushion upon which we remained suspended in the water. The entire submarine was now submerged, with the exception of ten feet of periscope protruding incongruously from the centre of the basin. We were down.

'From for'ard, sir. Fore hatch leaking badly.'

Bloody exaggeration! If the leak is a bad one, we'd be down by the bows – and we aren't.

'Tell 'em to clip it tighter.' *They'll have to get used to piddling little leaks – and to bigger ones!* But dark, weather-beaten Archie Baxter, the foreman from Vickers', leapt forward to give his advice.

While half the ship's company checked and counter-checked for signs of leaks, the remainder performed the tedious business of an inclining experiment to test stability. The sailors' part was to shift ten tons of pig iron from one part of the boat to another. After an hour and a half the job was done. We could go back up. 'Stand by to surface', I ordered.

'Check main vents', ordered Taylor.

'All main vents checked shut, sir', came the report.

I nodded, satisfied. 'Surface.'

'Blow One and Six main ballast tanks', Taylor called.

E.R.A. Lewis opened two of the direct blow valves. Air, at four thousand pounds per square inch, screamed through narrow steel pipes to the tanks at bow and stern, forcing out and replacing the water. We rose to the surface. Signalman Osborne opened the upper conning-tower hatch and I climbed out to the wet bridge.

Our first dive was behind us. If only every future dive would be as simple!

On January 28th, we received our sailing orders from the Naval Officer in Charge, Barrow-in-Furness: 'Proceed to Holy Loch under the escort of H.M.S. *Cutty Sark.*'

Lieutenant Taylor and I arranged to see our families in Scotland, but for the rest of the crew the sailing order meant all the embarrassing false gaiety of last good-byes. No one knew, or dared to speculate, when they would come back, how they would come back – or if they would come back at all. But there were brave smiles, gallant assurances and confident promises.

The morning was bleak and grey, and the wind played a

merry game with our commissioning pennant and White Ensign. The local gates opened and we saw the escort vessel, *Cutty Sark*, standing out to sea. The wires securing us to the dock were let go, and as we gathered way the bows were buffeted by saucy, dancing waves. We raised our hands to the men who built her, and they replied with a lusty cheer.

'Give 'em hell, skipper!'

'You bet we will!'

In Morecambe Bay we dipped to the swell. White-flecked sea surged angrily over the casing, splashing spray on to the bridge. The first voyage of the *Unbroken* was going to be a rough one.

As we passed the north of the Isle of Man the full force of the gale struck us on the port beam, and the *Unbroken* rolled considerably in the short, heavy swell. There were only three of us on the bridge – myself and the two look-outs – and with good reason. In a crash-dive you start to go down immediately the klaxon sounds, and you permit yourself only fifteen seconds in which to submerge. These fifteen seconds allow just enough time for three men on the bridge to get below and close the hatches above them before the boat goes under. If there were more than three men trying to get below, the conning-tower hatches would still be open as the submarine went down, the control-room would be half-flooded, and it would be the devil of a job to secure the hatches against the inrush of water. (There were to be times when the *Unbroken* completed the operation in twelve seconds!) Consequently, when a request was sent over the voice-pipe for one of the A.B.s to come up to the bridge to be sick, I replied: 'Certainly not. Give him a bucket.' I discovered later that this was considered harsh and even brutal, although for the life of me, I don't see why. After all, the *Unbroken* was a submarine at war, not the *Saucy Sue* giving sixpenny rides round the lighthouse. The inconvenience of one man being seasick was hardly measurable against the security of an entire ship's company.

It was dark by the time we sailed into the Clyde estuary,

guided by the shaded blue stern light of the *Cutty Sark*. We spent the night alongside the depôt ship, *Forth*, in Holy Loch, and in the reluctant, cinereous Greenock dawn, moved round to the famous submarine testing water of the Gareloch.

Diving trials followed, first at comparatively slow speeds, then at full speed - in our case eight-and-a-half knots. At that speed, when the hydroplanes give the submarine a stomach-turning tilt, it takes but a few seconds to dive from periscope depth to ninety feet – and, if you are not on your toes, only a few seconds more to dive from ninety feet to hull-splitting disaster on the bottom. Throughout the day the trials continued. We dived to periscope depth and worked up to full speed. I gave the order: 'Hard-a-dive on both hydroplanes', and the submarine tilted to an angle of fifteen degrees, bows down. This might not sound a very acute angle, but in a submarine heading for the bottom at speed, it is. Down . . . down . . . down, until the hydroplanes were reversed and we hoped to God she would pull out of the dive. She did, every time – and we sent our silent thanks to the men of Barrow.

On the voyage back to Holy Loch I signed a chit accepting delivery of one complete submarine. The thought struck me that it was very decent of the Admiralty to allow a mere lieutenant to sign their receipt to Vickers for a ship that must have cost them something in the region of a quarter of a million pounds. On the other hand, of course, I was accepting her at my own risk.

Trials, trials and more trials until, in mid-February, we went to Arrochar at the top of Loch Long for the final trial, testing our torpedo-tubes. Here Lieut. Taylor and I were to spend the last four days with our families. It was a happy interlude.

On the afternoon before sailing, Sub-Lieutenant John Haddow, the armament officer, accompanied Ting and me on a picnic tea by the shores of Loch Lomond. Before we returned to Arrochar we lay on the sands and sipped Loch

Lomond water, observing the local superstition that it would bring us luck. At eight o'clock next morning Ting walked to the pier with me. The *Unbroken* lay only a hundred yards off shore, a low, grey shape against the snow-covered mountains. There was little we could say that was not better left unsaid. Wartime farewells – as so many of us know – are profoundly upsetting moments over which it is better not to linger. Ting was obviously distressed, while I felt a pang of regret that I would not see my child, due to be born any day.

'I won't think much of you if you don't come back', she said.

I gave an easy salute, turned, and boarded the motor boat that was to take me to the *Unbroken*. As we cast off, Ting's 'Cheerio' echoed across the water.

On February 20th, as we sailed into the calm waters of Holy Loch, I received the signal: 'Daughter born yesterday. Both doing well.' Forty-eight hours later the *Unbroken*, a minute fragment of Britain at war, sailed south to 'seek out and destroy the enemy wherever he may be found'.

CHAPTER

1

CAPE ST VINCENT disappeared into the sea astern, and we set course past Cadiz for Cape Trafalgar. Within forty-eight hours we would be at Gibraltar.

Ten-thirty. The ward-room was dark and silent. I un-buttoned the collar of my jacket and stretched out on the settee that served as my bed. Sleep was elusive, and as I lay there, restless and ill-tempered, I became strangely con-scious of the sounds around me; noises that were normally so much an essential background to submarine life they were never heard nor noticed – the dominant clatter of the engines, an occasional voice, the scrape of a boot against an iron ladder, the apologetic shuffle of slippers through the ward-room. Percolating through them all the angry moan of the sea as it swished past our sides. For the first time in many years I became aware, too, of the strange smell peculiar to submarines: the curious combination of oil and damp and gas that dries the mouth and lines the throat.

I twisted on the hard, unyielding cushions and wished we were at Gibraltar where there would be mail from home – news of my wife and the daughter I had not seen. June. We had agreed to call her that. I wondered whom she re-sembled, and hoped Ting had left hospital to join her aunt at Aldeburgh. I wondered what was happening back in England, and how Paul Skelton and Tubby Linton were getting on – and then there was no time to wonder about anything. . . .

'Night alarm!' The voice of Taylor boomed down the voice-pipe into the control-room.

What the devil's this? As the order was relayed through the boat by alarm buzzer, I leapt from the settee, grabbed my glasses from the table, slithered across the control-room and climbed to the bridge. I heard Taylor order a change of course. The moon was high and to the south, the sea was glass-smooth, there was hardly any wind. Taylor was leaning over the voice-pipe. He turned towards me. 'Darkened ship on port bow, sir. I'm altering course to intercept.' To the voice-pipe: 'Midships . . . Steady!'

From the helmsman below: 'Course, sir, oh-seven-oh.'

Taylor raised his glasses. 'There she is now, sir, bearing green three-oh.'

I levelled my glasses parallel to his. In the bottom half of the lenses the blackness of the sea; in the top half the dark grey of the cloud-filled night. Between, on the sharply defined line of the horizon, the smudge of a small ship without lights. I thought at once of the warning we had received that 'Q' ships – armed trawlers masquerading as innocent fishermen – were lurking in the area. According to the law of things they should not have been able to operate so far from home, but it appeared that Vichy France or the Spanish were permitting the Germans secret use of their ports. A serious menace to Allied shipping, a 'Q' trawler was quite a handful for a small submarine to tackle. Equipped with both Asdic and depth charges, she carried a gun that out-ranged our own, while her defence against submarines was the knowledge that her short length made her a difficult torpedo target. Since we did not expect to meet friendly forces until the next day, the ship on the horizon might well be such a vessel. The odds were not altogether against us, however. With naval radar little more than a good idea on a drawing-board, we might be able to creep to within a thousand yards, pump ten quick shells into her, or try our luck with a torpedo. . . .

Taylor 'trimmed down' – order the flooding of numbers Two, Three, Four and Five main ballast tanks so that we rode on the air contained in numbers One and Six only. This caused us to settle in the water, reducing our silhouette, and also kept us ready for a quick dive.

'Gun action stations', I ordered.

The five men of the gun's crew, who had mustered at the foot of the conning-tower when 'Night Alarm' was sounded, clattered to the bridge and climbed over to the gun platform. Smoothly, quickly, silently, they unlocked the gun and unclipped the watertight ready-use lockers with their ten rounds of ammunition. Haddow, the armament officer, who would direct the fire of the gun, had already joined me on the bridge with Signalman Osborne. The ammunition party closed up to form a human chain from the magazine to the gun. Haddow leaned over to the gun platform. 'Bearing green three-oh. . . . A ship . . . Range oh-three-oh . . . Deflection twelve left . . . With H.E., *load*!' The gun swung on its mounting. 'Gun ready!' Haddow reported. 'Ready to open fire, sir.'

'Very good.'

Silence. We waited, tense. I felt certain the others could hear my heart thumping against my ribs. The seconds dragged by. As we neared each other, there was no mistaking that the unknown vessel was a trawler. *Well, you so and so, can you see us or not?*

From the control-room: 'All tubes ready.'

From the Asdic operator: 'H.E. green two-five . . . Single screw ship . . . Reciprocating engine . . . Ninety revs.' This confirmed she was a trawler, and told me additionally that she was approaching us at nine knots.

'Osborne, make the single letter challenge.'

The Aldis lamp stabbed a thick beam in the direction of the direction of the trawler. 'Challenge made, sir.'

No reply. Again we challenged – and again. Still no reply.

Was she trying to lure us closer? By rights we should open fire.

'In international code, tell her to stop.'

We were near enough now for the flashing of the Aldis lamp to illuminate the trawler like a miniature searchlight. She looked British.

If it's one of ours what the hell are they up to? Or is it really an enemy ship playing clever? We're only a thousand yards off her, and she could massacre us with machine guns. . . . 'Haddow!'

'Sir?'

'Fire one round across her bows.'

With a flash and a roar, a 3-inch shell screamed through the air, pitched some two hundred yards ahead of the trawler's bows and ricocheted into space.

It served its purpose: an immediate reply came to our challenge. To confirm, we again challenged and again received the correct reply. So she *was* British, but I was in no mood to extend a big hullo. For one thing, I was furious with the operational staff at Gibraltar who had not bothered to inform me of the trawler's presence in the area; for another I was anything but impressed by the trawler's look-outs and her delay in answering my signal. My immediate feeling was that she had deserved to be sunk.

We altered course to pass under her stern. As we did so, a great cloud of smoke billowed from the trawler's funnel. She, too, was altering course – straight towards us!

She's going to ram us! 'Stand by to dive . . . Full ahead together . . . Fire a night grenade.'

In the light of the recognition firework the gun's crew, signalman and look-outs scampered below followed by Haddow. I was alone on the bridge with Taylor. 'She'll depth-charge us if we dive', he said.

'My God, I believe she would.'

Then, without warning, the trawler's gun flashed and a shell screamed over our heads. Again she fired.

We were in a real mess. If we stayed on top she'd blow us out of the water. If we dived she would depth-charge us.

Yet she was British – unless the enemy had got hold of our recognition signals. I thought quickly. 'Signalman on the bridge', I yelled.

Osborne climbed through the conning-tower hatch, Aldis in hand, lead trailing behind.

'Make the rudest two-word signal you can think of.'

The Aldis beamed across the water. 'Done, sir.'

Yes, the trawler was British for, as though obeying Osborne's impolite signal, she altered course away from us. As she did so there burst forth one, then two great flares which slowly parachuted down to the sea. The trawler had fired star shells. This was the most extraordinary piece of stupidity I had come across in many a long day. We had been quite visible to the trawler, and the star shells served no purpose save to attract every U-boat within a radius of thirty miles. I relieved my feeling by giving the trawler's captain a severe bottle before sending him about his business. (On arrival at Gibraltar I discovered he was senior to me, but he apologised for the incident, none the less. I learned also that he shot down a Focke Wulf during his patrol, and I could not resist asking: 'What with? Star shells?')

Order restored, I returned to the ward-room. Haddow was there already. 'Well,' I said, 'you've fired your first round in anger.'

Ever the good armament officer, he shook his head. 'Waste of a damn good round, sir', he complained.

As I sat on the edge of the settee, I was overcome with an unaccountable weariness. It was not so much the excitement of the past forty-five minutes – for it was only that short period since Taylor had ordered 'Night Alarm' – as a tremendous sense of anticlimax. I felt vaguely cheated, and made to look silly. I muttered a curse that embraced the whole world, lay back, and was soon asleep.

I had yet to realise that commanding a submarine was one long series of frustrations and anticlimax, punctuated only occasionally by the thrill of positive achievement.

27

If it served no other purpose, the encounter with the trawler provided the crew with a fresh topic of conversation, and gave new animation to the interminable games of solo, cribbage and ukkers in the messes. Routine life aboard a submarine is a dull, monotonous business. You eat, sleep, test and exercise; read, argue and write letters home; speculate and reminisce – and all the time the air becomes heavier and more sour, tempers grow short and nerves are frayed, and you curse the day you ever volunteered to serve in these caricatures of sardine tins. Yet, with human perversity, you know deep down in your heart you would not be elsewhere. . . .

It may seem strange, but although it was now three months since they had joined the *Unbroken*, and although we were living in the closest proximity, I knew very little about my officers. There was a certain reticence, as though we realised that the time would come when we would share one communal soul in which nothing was secret. Aware of this in some indefinable way, we held ourselves back, as though to delay that final moment of truth.

John Haig Haddow I knew better than the others, of course, for he had served in my training submarine – a hazel-eyed Scot, barely twenty-one years old, very tall and willowy, with an undemonstrative toughness that was often mistaken for softness, and a great sense of humour. Taylor, plump and jolly, was some three years older than myself, a reservist from the Merchant Navy. Paul Thirsk, the navigator, was also a reservist: tall, blond, handsome and twenty-three years old. Later, Peter Churchill summed him up admirably when he said: 'Thirsk is the type of man you would like your sister to marry.' Women did, indeed, fall for him by the score, but he spurned them all and devoted his passion to the care and maintenance of an ancient check golfing jacket which he always wore when on watch. He claimed it brought him luck.

We were still comparative strangers, even though we lived, ate and slept together in a ward-room that measured no more than seven feet by nine – including two feet of passageway for people passing from for'ard to aft. Our beds consisted of two settees and two bunks, while lockers beneath the settees completed our austere furnishings. Not that the sailors were better off, of course. Some were lucky enough to have settees on which to sleep, others slung hammocks, while the remainder had to bed down as best they could in the for'ard torpedo-room.

The discipline of routine dominated our topsy-turvy lives – the routine of a day which scheduled breakfast at 10 a.m. and the midday meal at eight in the evening, and which did not permit us to see daylight and sunshine save through the end of a periscope. We dived at dawn and surfaced at dusk, and it was only during the hours of darkness, when the submarine was illuminated by the dull glow of dim red lighting that we were able to smoke, stretch our legs over a tot of rum and pause to reflect upon the unhappy life of those who served in surface vessels. Even so, despite the feeling of well-being that followed the heavy dinner cooked by Able Seaman Bramhall in his cubbyhole of a galley, there was no real slackening of pace. The ship was divided into three watches – red, white and blue – each doing two hours on and four off. While those off watch were able to sleep and sigh over their pin-ups, there was plenty of work for those on duty. Propelled on the surface by our diesels, an E.R.A. and two stokers stood guard over a thousand moving parts in the steel jungle of our engine-room. The main electric batteries had to be recharged, while cylinders were refilled with the compressed air that enabled us to surface. Men were on watch by the pumps, torpedo-tubes and cooling machinery. The wireless office received and decoded signals. An electrical rating toured the boat checking and testing battery readings. On the bridge, an officer and two ratings scanned sea and sky, while a helmsman, Asdic operator, Petty Officer of the Watch, duty E.R.A., messenger and 'spare hand' were crowded into a control-room hardly bigger than a garden shed.

None the less, for a submarine at sea in wartime we were as relaxed as ever we could be.

It was a fine, calm day when the *Unbroken* approached the Pillars of Hercules, slipped into Algeciras Bay and glimpsed Gibraltar town nestling at the foot of the fortress. In the foreground the familiar long grey moles of the artificial harbour. Alongside the moles the ships of Force H: the old battle-cruiser *Renown*, the battleship *Rodney*, the aircraft carrier *Eagle*, and a handful of destroyers. In the southern corner of the basin, by the dry docks, the submarine depôt ship *Maidstone*, our temporary home. This small force was all we had with which to defend the Western Mediterranean and a large slice of the Atlantic against all comers – German, Italian, and, if need be, Vichy French.

I felt we made a brave sight as we entered harbour. Our grey paint had held, and a brand new ensign, many sizes too large, flew from our tiny masthead. The sailors shared my pride in the occasion, and stood as stiff as Marines as they lined the casing in their bell-bottoms and white, roll-neck jerseys. We passed the towering sides of the *Renown*, *Rodney* and *Eagle*, bos'ns' pipes shrilling in salute, smug in the knowledge that despite their comparative enormity we could destroy any one of them with a minimum of effort. They, on the other hand, might never find, far less sink, us. Without their escorting destroyers they were powerless against a submarine – even against the undersized *Unbroken*, half the displacement of the average. For a young lieutenant it was a satisfying thought!

The *Maidstone*, to which we secured, was a floating dockyard equipped with torpedoes, ammunition, water, oil, food, spare parts and all the essentials for repair work. Aboard her were engineers, electricians, artificers, shipwrights, doctors and even a dentist; all with magnificently equipped workshops, foundries and surgeries. Little praise was ever given to the depôt ships, but our submarines – and thus the Mediterranean war – depended upon them to no small degree.

Business was slack aboard the *Maidstone* when we arrived. She had no flotilla of her own to mother, but acted as a sort of Clapham Junction for submarines entering and leaving the Med., travelling from England to Africa, and from Africa to England. She was responsible, also, for a couple of transport submarines running supplies to beleaguered Malta.

As I climbed the ladder up her side, I hoped we would be allowed one 'working up' patrol from Gib. before being sent into the Med., but Captain G. A. W. Voelcker, her Commanding Officer, had some shocks for me. As he paced his cabin, hands clasped behind his back, this lean, versatile captain, who was later to go down with the *Charybdis* in the Channel, looked serious and worried. What he told me amounted to this:

British submarines in the Mediterranean had, in some months, destroyed fifty per cent of the men, munitions and armour sent from Italy to the enemy forces in North Africa. The lion's share of this destruction was the work of the 10th flotilla based at Malta; a group of boats that boasted, among others, such commanders as Wanklyn, Tompkinson and Cayley. Their leader was that superb submarine strategist Captain (now Rear-Admiral) G. W. G. Simpson – 'Shrimp' Simpson as he was called with affectionate disrespect. No army could stand the losses that Rommel had suffered at the hands of the 10th flotilla. Consequently the submarine base at Malta had received the unremitting attention of the Italian and German air forces, and the point came when bombing caused so many casualties that the remnants of the flotilla had to flee to Alexandria. Our submarines out of the way, Rommel was building up the strength to launch what was to be his last great offensive.

(Later, he was to push the Desert Rats back to Egypt, capture Tobruk and Mersa Matruh and move close enough to threaten Alex. Once again the remnants of the 10th had to move, this time to Beirut. With them went the reduced 1st flotilla whose permanent home was at Alex. On the way to Beirut our largest depôt ship, the *Medway*, was sunk. Fortunately, half her store of torpedoes was sent ahead by land, otherwise submarine operations in the Eastern Med. would have come to a complete standstill.)

Even by April things were grim. The two submarines entering the Med. immediately before the *Unbroken*'s arrival at Gib. had both been sunk. Wanklyn and Tompkinson had been lost, and the sea bed was littered with our wrecks. The *Una*, commanded by Pat Norman, Harrison's 'P. 34', and the *Umbra*, commanded by Lynch Maydon, were the only submarines of the old 10th flotilla left – and they were at the far end. When the *Unbroken* arrived at Malta she would be the only submarine afloat in a heart-breaking scrap-yard of bomb- and mine-shattered hulks.

My immediate reaction to the news was to say: 'Well, let's sail for Malta right away and get cracking', but Captain Voelcker shook his head.

'No,' he said, 'you can't even get into the Grand Harbour at Valetta. Apart from his tremendous bombing effort on the island itself, the enemy has carried out a complete blockade by mining. The "searched channels" are absolutely blocked with every variety of mine that German and Italian ingenuity can devise. We don't even know how to sweep some of the more complicated ones. Even if we did, all our sweepers have been sunk! By an all-out effort of his Mediterranean air forces the enemy has managed to deny us the effective use of Malta. But as soon as he lets up, or as soon as we can get a few fighters in and operate them, your chance will come.'

With a long face and heavy heart I left him.

Two of the veterans of Malta, long overdue for home, had managed to stagger to Gib. where they were receiving temporary repairs before limping back to England. There was the Polish *Sokol*, commanded by Boris Karnicki. She had suffered terrible poundings, both at sea and at Malta, and it was a miracle that she made Gib. Teddy Woodward, commanding the *Unbeaten,* also crawled into Algeciras Bay on one battery, the other smashed by bombing.

Understandably, they were not anxious to discuss their experiences. The slaughter and the havoc were too vivid in their minds to be the subjects of chatty conversations. In any case there are some things it is better not to know.

March at Gibraltar is a dreary month, but we enjoyed it after the chill of a northern winter. A great attraction were the shops, piled high with all the ingredients of feminine allure – cosmetics, silk stockings, chocolates, dress lengths, scents, and dainty underwear. They had been exported from England, and while they would have satisfied only a minute portion of the home market, at Gibraltar they served to impress the Spanish that England was still a wealthy land of luxuries, and that 'starvation' stories to the contrary were nothing but enemy propaganda. We bought as much of it as we could afford, and sent it to England with pals on homeward-bound ships. The Customs at the other end did not seem to mind – unless some idiot started selling the stuff in the Black Market – and I had pleasing visions of a silk gowned Ting, the envy of Utility-frocked Aldeburgh.

I could only assume she was now at Aldeburgh. To our annoyance and disgust there was no mail awaiting us aboard the *Maidstone.* Something had gone wrong somewhere – one of those irritating mix-ups which every Serviceman experiences at some time or another, and which, although small in themselves, are vastly upsetting to the individual.

Apart from the ward-room aboard the *Maidstone,* there was plenty of gaiety at the Rock Hotel if you fancied 'poodle-faking'. As I remember, there was no less than four thousand Service officers permanently stationed at Gib. with no apparent purpose except to amuse a handful of Wrens. None of us in the *Unbroken* had the temerity to embark on such a passionate quest, for even the most ardent among us could not fail to notice that it was *de rigueur* to have

3

at least three stripes (or their Army or Air Force equivalent) on the arm that supported a popsy! The Wrens had lots of fun at Gib., and I have often wondered how they readjusted themselves when they returned to the comparatively dull routine of civilian life.

There was an eleven o'clock curfew at Gib., but when the crew of the *Unbroken* decided to throw a party at a local 'boiled-oil shop' they were certain the Provost-Marshal had not intended that they should be included in the regulation. Consequently they were to be seen returning to the dockyard in the early hours of the morning along a zigzag course any U-boat conscious skipper would have envied. The sudden personal appearance of the Provost-Marshal had a steadying and sobering effect, however. The songs died on their lips and they dispersed as fast as their legs could carry them. A few, who shall be nameless, climbed a tree and waited for the Provost-Marshal to pass. As he walked beneath the branches there was a breathless moment until one rating, discovering that wine-drinking and tree-climbing do not mix, was violently ill. Furious – and rightly so – the Provost-Marshal blew his whistle, and what seemed like an entire regiment of soldiers appeared from the neighbouring rocket sites. A merry game of hide-and-seek ensued before the sailors made their escape. We were then living in the spacious and comfortable quarters of the *Maidstone*, and with great ingenuity the celebrants managed to sneak aboard without falling foul of the officer of the watch. As none of them were caught, the Provost-Marshal did not discover from which ship the wrongdoers came, and I did not hear of the matter officially. I learned of it in dribs and drabs around the *Maidstone*, but thought it as well to turn the naval equivalent of a blind eye. Such things often happen, for Jack ashore is an uninhibited soul. Indeed, it will be a bad day when he is not.

The *Maidstone* was a tribute to the ingenuity of her designers, for despite her bulk, it seemed impossible for so many amenities to be crammed between her sides. From our point of view the most agreeable of these amenities was the living space provided for the officers and men of the submarines attached to her. While the sailors had large mess-decks in which to shake off their claustrophobia, the officers were given individual cabins, each a small 'bedsitter'. There were film shows and recreational facilities, too, but our life was hardly a giddy round of pleasure. No ship can be too efficient, and we spent our days, backed by technicians from the *Maidstone*, testing, checking, adjusting and oiling against the happy moment when I would order: 'Fire one!' and a 'kipper'* would tear through the sea towards an enemy vessel.

The ward-room of the *Maidstone* was almost empty, and I sipped a lonely horse's neck at the bar. I was depressed, and as I stared moodily at my glass I mourned the fact that I was having a bloody awful war. No adventure, excitement, amusement or feeling of usefulness. I reckoned I might just as well be at home with Ting as wasting the weeks in Gib. waiting for something to happen

My thoughts were interrupted by the appearance of a messenger. 'Excuse me, sir, but the captain would like to see you in his cabin.'

What's this? Another apologetic explanation for us not going to Malta? 'I'll be right along.' With a complete absence of enthusiasm I made my way aft.

Captain Voelcker was alone in his day cabin. He invited me to sit down.

'Well, Mars, you know you're the only submarine around these parts, don't you?' The question was purely rhetorical and I did not feel it needed an answer. He smiled. 'Know anything about folboats?'

'No, sir, except that they're canvas folding boats, like canoes.'

Voelcker nodded. 'There's a special operation for you in a week's time.' My heart raced. 'Utmost secrecy is essential. I

*Torpedo. ('Tin fish' is no longer used by sub-mariners.)

am telling you, and you alone, that it will involve landing people on the coast of France. You'll be away about a month and you'll land a party of four. Your job is to get them there and see they paddle ashore safely in their folboats. They've probably never seen a submarine before and will be a damned nuisance. That's too bad. Their leader is a bloke called Churchill.' He saw my expression and laughed. 'No, not that one! This is a Captain Peter Churchill. You'll meet him and his desperadoes later. In the meantime we've got some folboats and you can amuse yourself finding out how they work.' He smiled. 'That's all for the present.'

Cloak and dagger, eh? What a turn up for the book! I hurried back to my cabin and summoned Taylor.

'Number One, we must be ready for a patrol five days from now. It'll be a long one. Allow for a month, then add another fortnight for emergencies. You can count on having five passengers with us for at least half the time. We'll be carrying two folboats. There will be extra equipment, too. You'll have to find room for it all for'ard. This is no ordinary patrol. I don't know the details yet, but all measures must be taken to keep secret that it's spy stuff until the folboats come aboard. When that cat is out of the bag I'll have a word with the ship's company. In the meantime it's just between ourselves. Even Thirsk and Haddow aren't to know. O.K.?'

The gleam in Taylor's eyes told me that this was the sort of thing he'd been waiting for. 'Aye, aye, sir. Will be done.'

'Just one thing, Number One.'

'Yes, sir?'

'As this is our first real patrol, come and see me if any doubtful points crop up.'

'Certainly, sir. Where is it going to be, or shouldn't I ask?'

'Don't know myself yet.'

He strode off with great *élan*, anxious to get cracking.

I returned to the ward-room. There was little I could do now. The submarine was as 'worked up' as I could make her and I was reasonably satisfied. Except for planning the details of the job I could not assist in the boat's preparations. That was the responsibility of each department, with the first lieutenant answerable for the overall results.

I sent for Thirsk and Haddow. 'Like to go boating this afternoon?'

'Bit chilly for sailing, isn't it, sir?' said Haddow, doubtfully.

'Not really the weather at all', added Thirsk.

'Ah, but this is a different sort of sailing', I assured them. 'Folboats. Jolly interesting.'

Thirsk and Haddow looked at each other, unconvinced. The former screwed up his face. 'Be a bit blowy, sir', he ventured.

'Nonsense. This afternoon we'll collect a folboat from the depôt ship and try it out. I'm told it's quite fun.' They still appeared unimpressed. 'Consider it an order', I added.

That afternoon we took a three-seater folboat, in a dubious state of repair, round to Rosia Bay – a reminder of the balmier days of 1932 when I had swum there with the angel fish and trod in terror of the sea egg. We were the only bathers. Maybe everyone was busy, although I could not guess what at, or perhaps the bathing season had not officially opened.

Half a gale blew in from the Atlantic, which produced 'I told you so' expressions from Thirsk and Haddow, but I egged them on with a story to the effect that I'd often shot the rapids in Canada and that this was kid's stuff in comparison. As we rigged the folboat on a small mole, I thought the frame rather fragile for the boat's size, but we launched it, climbed in and paddled around in the sheltered water until we had mastered the thing. By this time Haig Haddow was shivering like a willowy babe in the wood, and I allowed him to retire. I thought a good way of testing the seaworthiness of the boat would be to go out to the rolling waters beyond the mole, and a reluctant Paul Thirsk came as my one-man crew.

We had travelled about a hundred yards beyond the protection of the mole when the contraption began to hog and sag as though its back was broken. When we finally turned towards shore I discovered that it did, indeed, suffer from this distressing defect, but I could not prevent it from rolling over and ditching us. Thirsk's blasphemy over the loss of a brand-new Ronson lighter, which had been lying at the bottom of the boat, was not softened by the certain knowledge that Haig Haddow was laughing his head off on the safe, dry mole. The sea was rougher and the current stronger than we thought, and it took us half an hour to manoeuvre the folboat back to safety. Politely Haig Haddow helped to haul the wreck to the beach, and refrained from comment. Paul Thirsk, however, could not resist remarking: 'Great stuff this boating, sir. How did you enjoy it?'

I have only been in one folboat since, and that was a different sort of skylark.

Joe Cowell, the *Maidstone*'s Staff Officer (Operations), introduced me to Peter Churchill. If I had expected him to be a blond, titanic Viking in the best traditions of the heroes of the twopenny bloods, I would have been disappointed. Of medium build, dark, and with deep, intelligent eyes, he would only be distinguishable in a crowd by his charm and a certain sense of authority. Here was a stronger character, I felt, unassuming and quiet, yet capable of decisive violence should the occasion arise.

In the cabin of Captain 'S' – Captain commanding the submarine flotilla – the plot was unfolded. We were to land four agents on the south coast of Vichy France, two at Antibes, and two at a suitable spot to be chosen by me. Churchill was to land with them but would return aboard. When this mission was completed, and not before, we were to have a few days' free-lance operations in the Gulf of Genoa – a little titbit for being good boys.

I was somewhat concerned about Antibes Bay. I recalled

school holidays there when plenty of fishing boats had been about. Perhaps all that had been changed by the war, but it was going to be a tricky problem getting in and out of the tiny bay none the less. There was little doubt that we would have to enter the bay, for my folboat experience had shown me that those canvas craft were suitable only for the shortest and calmest of journeys. But I held my peace, for these were problems that would have to be solved on the spot.

The need for secrecy was obvious. Everyone knew that we carried out clandestine ops against the enemy coast, but it would be suicide to have the Germans know in advance where the next one was going to be. I decided that without mentioning the matter to 'S' I would do a little scattering of red herrings.

The patrol orders with our destination cryptically labelled 'W.M.P. 13' in my pocket, I sent for Paul Thirsk. 'Tell me, old boy, have we the charts for the north-west African coast from here down to Sierra Leone?'

'No, sir. We've all the Med. charts, and our passage charts from Gib. to the U.K., and from Suez to Colombo and Mombasa.'

'Then arrange to draw these others from the dockyard. Have them delivered direct to the boat. Then check and correct them in the control-room.'

'Aye, aye, sir. But is it all right to be seen doing it?'

'I want you to be seen – but be as furtive as you can. Get it?'

Thirsk smiled. 'Aye, aye, sir.'

As we were the only fully operational submarine at Gib., preparing for the patrol was an easy task: the *Maidstone* was able to devote all her energies to us. The biggest single job was topping-up the main batteries. They came to about three thousand times the size of a large car battery and needed between fifty and a hundred gallons of distilled water. Torpedoes were prepared, diesel fuel and lubricating oil were taken aboard, also fresh water and food. The submarine service must have been Lord Woolton's pet, for our fridge and storeroom were always well stocked. Into them went eggs and bacon, butter and beef; lamb, pork, liver and mutton; cheese, corned beef, flour and tinned potatoes; tinned carrots, tomatoes, beetroots and fish; cocoa, soup, milk and fruit; tinned tongue and ham; dehydrated potatoes and fresh potatoes; and as much fresh salad as we could lay hands on. There was enough fresh, tinned and dehydrated food to last us a month, and we could survive for another two weeks on our supplies of ship's biscuits and 'corned dog'. As the food was hoisted aboard there were the usual arguments as to where it would all be stowed, and I knew that a sizeable portion of it would end up in the torpedo compartment, much to the annoyance of the ratings who slept there.

I could see that Number One was becoming anxious about our destination. 'Can you tell me where it's to be, sir?'

'I'm sorry, Taylor, but I'd better keep it under my hat.'

'Yes, sir. . . . Two folboats are being embarked this afternoon. Would you like to see the ship's company in the dinner-hour before the folboats arrive?'

'A good idea. Make it eleven-forty-five.'

'Yes, sir. There's one thing, sir, that worries me a little.'

'What's that, old boy?'

'There's a buzz going around that we're doing a patrol down the West African coast, Dakar way.'

'Is there now? Thanks for letting me know. I'll have a word to say about buzzes when I see the ship's company.'

Just before lunch the crew crowded into the control-room and overflowed into the passageways beyond. I reminded them how their lives depended in no small degree on secrecy. I told them about the folboats, and added: 'But don't start making wild speculations. They mean nothing. Folboats are a part of a submarine's equipment in the Med. Just the same, I don't want any mention made outside the boat of any special equipment we take aboard. It is not to be spoken of even in the depôt ship.' I concluded by warning them that rumour was a fickle jade liable to play them false.

After tea on April 11th, Peter Churchill and his party came aboard. As they were considered part of the boat's armament, Haddow attended to their needs. Churchill was allotted the fourth sleeping-place in the ward-room. This was practical, for although we numbered three officers apart from myself, one was always on watch at sea and came down to occupy the bunk of the chap who had relieved him. Thus one billet was always unoccupied. Churchill's four desperadoes were distributed among the petty officers' and seamen's messes, which meant even more overcrowding in the for'ard torpedo-room. The party's baggage, including certain weapons of sabotage, were taken aboard, and Haddow examined these latter items with the professional interest of an armament officer. It was as well that he did so, for included among them were pencil-bombs filled with plastic explosives and designed to be attached to aircraft. Operated on a barometer principle, they would explode when the aircraft reached a certain altitude and the air pressure decreased. The desperadoes did not realise it, but such drops in pressure occur in submarines, too, and the pencil-bombs might well have exploded during the voyage and made a very nasty mess. They were sent ashore far more quickly than they were brought aboard!

We were due to sail at five o'clock. I changed into my seagoing dress – old trousers, kapok jacket, towel-scarf, old cap and binoculars – and went to say *au revoir* to Captain Voelcker. As we chatted, Joe Cowell burst in.

'I'm sorry, sir, but Mars will have to wait. The "Pay" has gone ashore with the keys of the safe and we can't get the money. I've sent a car to bring him back.'

This was the first I'd heard of any money, and shortly afterwards an apologetic Supply Officer arrived with four black silk body-belts. Each contained a million francs. And so, with four million francs tucked beneath my arm, I crossed the plank to the *Unbroken* and climbed to the bridge.

'Ready for sea', Taylor reported.

'All right. We're off.'

I handed the loot to Thirsk. 'Nip down and lock this in the ward-room safe, will you?'

I looked for'ard and aft. The plank had been withdrawn and we were secured to the *Maidstone* by single wires at bow and stern.

'Group up . . . Let go.'

The wires splashed into the oily water of the harbour.

'Main motors ready grouped up, sir', said a voice from below.

'Half astern together.'

We slid away from the *Maidstone*. A wave from Captain Voelcker. . . . More waves. . . . '*Bon voyage*' from Joe Cowell. Through Algeciras Bay into the centre of the Strait. Curious watchers on the Spanish shore saw us sail south-west in the gathering dusk. Out of sight of their prying eyes we swung around to east-north-east.

We entered the Mediterranean.

2

It was quite dark now, and we remained surfaced. I told
Paul Thirsk to set a zigzag course to pass west of Majorca
and into the Gulf of Lions, and stayed a while on the bridge
before handing over to Taylor who was officer of the watch.
The night was cool and quiet, its flat nigrescence broken
only by the dull glow of a small forest fire on the Spanish
mainland. We might have been on a routine exercise in
peacetime, for in the tranquil darkness it was difficult to
realise that ahead of us at Malta the skies were torn with the
scream of bombs and the furious bark of anti-aircraft guns;
that beyond Malta towards Alex. the seas were being
churned into foaming fury by the death agonies of our
shattered convoys; that the sands of Africa to the south-east
were crimson with the blood of the Eighth Army. It all
seemed very remote and a little unreal. It was difficult to
grasp, too, that in a week's time we would be nosing into the
hostile waters of Antibes Bay to land saboteurs and spies. I
did not envy our passengers their task, for while success
might mean some transient glory, failure meant the rubber
truncheon and a firing squad. For us, death would be
relatively clean. Why, I wondered, do people volunteer for
such jobs? Was it some fiery patriotism? Sense of duty?
Fatalistic indifference? Desire for adventure or gain? A
glorious madness? Perhaps, I reasoned, it was a little of all
those things, or may be it was none of them – that it was

considered a job of work that had to be done; no more, no less.

I went below to take a closer look at them.

Defying all known laws, the five had squeezed themselves into the ward-room together with Haddow and Thirsk. Peter Churchill greeted me with a winning smile. 'The gallant gentlemen are rather nervous', he said.

'I don't blame 'em', I replied. 'If I was going to paddle ashore at Antibes I'd be nervous, too. Bloody terrified, in fact.'

Churchill laughed. 'It isn't that that's worrying them. It's this submarine of yours. They don't like the idea of diving and surfacing. I've assured them there's hardly any sense of movement, but they don't seem very comforted. However, let me introduce you.'

I shook hands first with Jean, a silent Breton of doleful countenance who spoke no English and whose French seemed confined to the phrases: '*Veux manger . . . Veux dormir . . . Veux fumer . . . Soif.*' During the voyage we were able to satisfy his needs so far as eating and sleeping were concerned – he did little else, in fact – but he was most upset when we told him he simply could not smoke every time the fancy took him. 'Self-control!' Haddow would cry, but the Breton merely curled his lips and looked more woebegone than ever. On such occasions, however, a tot of rum worked wonders.

The second desperado was Léon, a tall, sharp-eyed Englishman who looked Spanish and spoke perfect French. The third was Bill, also English, and also bi-lingual; a short, cheerful little man whose subsequent conversations suggested that his pre-war occupation was connected with the white-slave traffic. The fourth member of the party must have been a very good agent indeed, for I cannot remember a single thing about him!

Not that there was much to be remembered of the others, either, for they disclosed little about themselves – a tribute, no doubt, to their excellent training – and we considered it wiser not to ask questions. Consequently our chatter was confined to amiable small talk, punctuated by anecdotes from Peter Churchill. He was a great raconteur and spent most of the voyage taking our minds from our duties with an endless flow of stories.

The days passed, and domestic life aboard the *Unbroken* kept to its routine pattern. To help break the dull sameness of the days, and to keep the crew up to scratch, I gave them plenty of exercises – dummy attacks, gun-drill, rehearsals in damage control, and change-round positions in which everyone learned to do everyone else's jobs. Our passengers thought it all highly amusing – until I exercised emergency increases in depth without warning them to hold on to their stomachs.

One morning I spotted Bill banging the sides of his hands furiously against the control-room ladder. 'What on earth is that for?' I asked.

He held both hands. 'Feel', he invited.

I did so. From the outsides of his little fingers to the wrists the skin was as hard and horny as tough leather. 'Banging them helps to harden them', said Bill. With one hand he cut the air in a short, sharp arc. 'The Judo chop', he explained. 'You can kill a man that way.' He grinned and returned to his banging.

By this time beards were beginning to sprout, including a delicate golden glow on the chin of Haig Haddow, and a remarkable growth on the thin Irish face of Chief E.R.A. Leslie Manuel – a sharply-pointed affair with fierce moustaches which gave him the appearance of a disreputable Spanish grandee who had known better days. As there was only one tiny wash-basin for the ratings, a second for the chief and petty officers, and a third for the wardroom, it can be understood why so many sub-mariners grew beards: it took long enough queueing to wash and clean your teeth, let alone shave. Since I did not favour a beard myself, and was fussy about regular shaving, my smooth cheeks, coupled with my rather elaborate kapok jacket, earned me a slanderous nickname among the sailors, which I overheard only by chance – 'Pansy'. It was also by chance that I overheard the nickname the crew had given Haddow. Capitalising on his tall, thin frame they called him 'Dip rod'. For a reason I could never make out, they dubbed Taylor 'Boogly-Woogly', while Thirsk as navigator was simply 'Navvy' or 'Pilot'.

It had been a very surprised crew that found us steering east from Gib. instead of west, so I told them over the Tannoy broadcast system what our real plans were, although I omitted to disclose the actual spot of disembarkation. Not that I mistrusted them in terms of keeping a secret – in any case, to whom could they disclose the information? – but I reckoned that if a man was unfortunate enough to become a P.O.W., the less he knew the better. As for the *Maidstone* and Gibraltar, they thought we were somewhere in the neighbourhood of Dakar. I felt very pleased with my little ruse.

Slowly we made our way north-west. Cartagena . . . Cape Palos . . . Alicante . . . Cape San Antonio . . . the Gulf of Valencia. Here we were greeted by half a gale, and as the *Unbroken* rolled like a drunken porpoise, our passengers turned green and took to their bunks. Apart from the mess and their personal discomfort, they caused Churchill and myself no little worry for they needed to be at the peak of condition when they were landed. Churchill fluttered round them like a clucking hen. To make matters worse the heavy seas were slowing us down, and we were in danger of being late for the rendezvous with the agents ashore. Our orders allowed for one postponement of twenty-four hours, but only one.

I stood on the hail-battered bridge with Taylor, cursing and blasting the weather, while the crackling electric flashes of St Elmo's Fire danced a lively jig on our periscope standard and aerials, lighting us up like a Christmas tree from bow to stern. It was as well the weather prevented

46

enemy aircraft from patrolling the area.

'We must press on', I yelled to Taylor. 'We've got to make up this lost time.'

'She's bumping badly, sir', he shouted back. 'Rolling a lot, too.' The words entered my ear mixed up with a gallon of spray.

'Yes', I replied. 'Can't be helped, though.'

'Very uncomfortable for'ard. Torpedoes may break loose.'

'Shouldn't do. Not if they're properly secured. Pass the word for the T.G.M.* to inspect them. It's not really rough. We're just pitching into it a bit. That's all.'

As I uttered the words we came out of the lee of the Balearic Islands and a violent, savage sea crashed against our side. A huge wall of water poured over the bridge.

'You'll have to slow down, sir', Taylor bawled. 'You're breaking her up.'

I was certain the thunderous noise of the sea was playing tricks with my hearing. '*What?*'

To my astonishment, he repeated his opinion. *He must be out of his mind. What blasted impertinence!* 'Don't worry about the boat. I can do that. I've been through a Pacific typhoon in a submarine and know something of their strength. We continue at the same speed.'

At that moment the last of St Elmo's Fire was swept away, and in its final sparkle I glimpsed a doubtful expression on Number One's face. I nodded to him. 'Good night, and don't forget we'll need starsights in the morning if there's any break in the cloud.'

Taylor nodded back. 'The Pilot knows about it, sir. Good night.'

I went below with mixed feelings. On the one hand I felt guilty at leaving Taylor on the bridge in introspective solitude during a gale, while on the other hand I was furious at what I considered his confounded cheek. *Has he forgotten I'm the Captain? How dare he accuse me of breaking-up the boat?*

* Torpedo Gunner's Mate.

47

I was particularly upset because this was not the first difference we had had, and even the suggestion of bad feeling is fatal among a small group of men living in such proximity as we were. Stretched out on my settee, I tried to persuade myself that it was a storm in a teacup, a fraying of tempers that had been aggravated by the thunder of the night and which would blow over with the coming of the dawn. None the less I did sleep easily.

At noon on April 19th I peered through the attack periscope into the semicircle of Antibes Bay. It is a little bay, for the rocks flanking it lie only half a mile apart, and the town of Antibes hiding in the northern corner gives the overall scene the effect of having been constructed solely for the picture-postcard trade. A light breeze stirred the gentlest of ripples on the placid blue water, and there was not even a rowing boat in sight to cause me alarm. It appeared that Peter Churchill had been right when he promised no fishing boats. Satisfied, I ordered courses that took us in a large, slow circle, and summoned Haddow, Taylor and Thirsk to join Churchill and myself in the ward-room. Briefly I outlined my plan.

'Tonight we'll approach the bay from eastward and creep in to within seven hundred yards of the spot where Churchill wants to land. This cuts to the minimum the distance he has to travel. His job is a tricky one, and since his pals know nothing about folboats they'll be a dead weight on his hands.

'For our part, we have no navigational aids, such as small lighthouses, to guide us. We'll choose some handy rocks on the chart, and guide ourselves in by getting Asdic ranges and bearing from them. All right so far?' I scanned their eager faces. They nodded. 'Good. Thirsk. You will steer her in from below on Cryer's Asdic bearings. I'll keep a visual look-out on the bridge. Haddow will be with me as officer of the watch. Taylor, you will be on the casing to supervise the embarkation. Lee, the T.G.M., will be responsible for getting the folboats in and out of the for'ard hatch, and he'll also be responsible for shutting the hatch in a hurry if the need arises.

'In the position I've chosen, we'll be only four hundred yards from the nearest rocks, but I'm taking the chance that no one will be standing there with binoculars at one in the morning! Since we'll be end-on to the shore and trimmed down, I don't think we can be seen without binoculars. Any questions?'

There were none. 'The plan is', I continued, 'that Churchill will go ashore in one of the folboats and make contact with his pals there. By the time he returns we'll have his two desperadoes waiting in the second folboat. Off they go together, Churchill will guide his friends to the agents ashore, then return to the submarine towing the second folboat behind him. Churchill will then make one more trip to take ashore the remainder of the equipment. That's all there is to it.'

The conference broke up. I was glad the planning part of our operation was over, and looked forward to a little excitement and action. But 'the best-laid schemes of mice and men gang aft a-gley' when the elements become capricious, and with the setting of the sun the mistral swept down the valley of the Var from the Alps, the sky lowered, and rain squalls lashed the sea. This was not going to help the launching of the folboats. None the less, we would have to take a chance, and with a melodramatic accompaniment of thunder claps and the flashing of vivid blue lightning, we surfaced.

As we closed Antibes I stood on the bridge with Haddow and Churchill. The rain poured down. It was eleven o'clock. The operation was due to start at midnight. As the minutes crawled past we stood in gloomy silence, until Haddow remarked: 'I think it's easing up, sir.'

'I doubt it', I said, and tried to stamp the water from my shoes.

But Haddow was right. As suddenly as it had started the

squall died away, the wind dropped and the night was clear again.

'Thank goodness for that', said Churchill.

'Yes', I replied dully.

'You don't seem very enthusiastic', he complained.

'I'm not. Look.' I pointed into the darkness. On the port beam was the unmistakable silhouette of a darkened boat. *A damn nuisance, a damn bloody nuisance!* 'I don't want anyone reporting our presence here, and I can't make a noise with the gun . . . I think I'll ram the bastard. Haddow! Alter course to intercept.'

As Haddow crossed to the voice-pipe and ordered the alteration of course, and as I continued to curse and blast the presence of the boat – which had no right to be darkened if a neutral – Churchill grabbed my arm. 'I've just remembered something', he said. 'That boat looks like a Spanish felucca, doesn't it? When we were at Gibraltar I was told a felucca would be landing some of our chaps somewhere on this part of the coast. It's a wild possibility, but supposing that's them? We can't sink them, can we? Nor can we take a chance.'

'Damn them at Gibraltar! Why the hell didn't they tell me?'

As Churchill muttered something about 'Security' I leaned over the voice-pipe and ordered a return to our original course towards the bay. But the damage had been done, for as we swung round another squall overtook us and Thirsk's voice came up from the control-room.

'Something wrong somewhere, sir. The echo-sounding machine is giving depths which don't check with those of the chart. We're somewhere off course. I'm a bit lost.'

'Either that or the echo-sounder's gone haywire.'

'Yes, sir.'

'Send up a party to take sounding with a hand lead and line from the casing.'

'Aye, aye, sir.'

Within a matter of seconds the sounding party appeared

through the conning-tower and made their way for'ard. Impatiently I drummed my fingers on the steel framework of the bridge.

'Seven fathoms, sir.'

'*Eh?* Check it.' *Seven fathons? I'm trying to discover whether its seventy or seventeen! Now everything's gone haywire.* . . . 'Well?'

'Seven fathoms, sir.'

I crossed to the voice-pipe. 'Thirsk! They report seven fathoms.'

'*Seven?*'

'Yes.'

'We *are* lost!'

Indeed we were. It was an incredible situation. Despite all our learning, contraptions and gadgets, despite our technical knowledge, charts and machines, the sea had tricked us.

I made a quick decision.

'Listen, Churchill, we've twenty-four hours in hand, and the weather's against us, anyway. I'm going to call it off for tonight. Haddow! Alter course away, and we'll stooge around until tomorrow night.'

'Aye, aye, sir.'

Feeling a complete idiot I went below. My only consolation, for what it was worth, was the knowledge that I had been proved right in pressing ahead despite the weather on the journey up.

We spent the next day dived some miles south of Nice. At last the sun sank below the horizon and the darkness of night crept over the water. Fortunately the weather held and the sky was clear when we surfaced. Three miles from Antibes I stopped the engines lest their noise should betray us to those on shore, and switched to the motors. We slid towards the bay in deep and utter silence.

Haddow was with me on the bridge, tin-hatted, a revolver at his side. He surveyed my own helmet and revolver and glanced at the two look-outs armed in a similar manner. 'Proper warlike, aren't we?' he whispered.

'Yes', I replied, 'but with this particular job to do, the last things we want to hear are the guns of war.'

'Too bloody true, sir.'

Slowly we approached the rocks into the open entrance of the bay. To my horror I saw that the entire foreshore was ablaze with twinkling lights!

'Stop both!'

The main motor switches were broken and the propellers stilled.

What the hell's this? Were they expecting us? . . . But they can't have been. . . . I swung my glasses. 'I've got it!'

'What is it, sir?' asked Haddow.

'Fishing boats, that's what they are.'

'Why the lights?' he asked.

'It's a trick of fishermen the world over. They're using acetylene flares to attract the fish. It's not as bad as it looks.' I crossed to the voice-pipe. 'My compliments to Captain Churchill and ask him to come to the bridge.'

He was with me in no time at all.

'Well, old boy, that's Intelligence, that is. Take an eyeful. Your blasted bay is littered with fishing boats and the whole place is lit up like a Brock's benefit.'

He gazed thoughtfully through my glasses, then turned towards me. He seemed nervous. 'Well?' he asked.

'Oh, you'll be able to get in all right.' I hoped I sounded as casual as I intended.

'Quite', he replied. 'However, I want to get out as well as in.'

'Ever come across these illuminated boats before?'

'No.'

I swallowed and when I spoke I did so with a tremendous effort at calmness. 'In that case you'll have to take my word for it that they can't see a damn thing. They're as blind as bats except for a radius of a yard or so from their flares. In shipping routes these fellows are literally a flaming menace. They can't even see a fully lighted ship approaching them. You'll be able to slip between them in your canoe without being spotted. As you go by there'll be enough light by which to thread a needle or read a book. But for God's sake trust me and take my word that *they'll be too blinded by light to see you.*'

'Are you quite sure?'

'Absolutely.'

A pause.

'All right, I'll try it.'

'Good show.' I relaxed and realised I was sweating like a pig. I must have put all I had into convincing Churchill that I was not sending him into the gaping jaws of death! 'We'll get the folboats up, shut the hatch, trim down to reduce sihouette and sneak in as per plan.'

I was beginning to enjoy myself again. 'Diving stations', I ordered. 'Stand-by gun action!' The ship's company flew to their posts; the gun's crew closed up at the foot of the conning-tower.

'Control-room.'

'Sir.'

'Tell the T.G.M. to let the bridge know when he's ready to open the fore hatch and get the boats up.'

'Message passed for'ard, sir.'

'Very good. Ask the navigator to speak on the voice-pipe.'

'Navigator speaking.'

'Pilot, give me the course to close our position. Come up here and get a land fix first. There's plenty in sight at present.'

Thirsk's tall figure blocked my view of the shore as he took his bearings with methodical precision. Typically, he did not waste time inquiring about the lights blazing off shore. Such chit-chat could come later.

Number One's voice floated up the voice-pipe. 'All ready for'ard, sir.'

'Thank you. Man the gun!'

The gun's crew rattled up the conning-tower ladder and hustled through to the gun platform. At the same time ratings manned the two Vickers' guns on the bridge.

'Number One. Come up now with the folboat party.' As his head rose through the conning-tower I ordered: 'Open fore hatch. Up folboats.'

While the folboats were coaxed through to the casing we were as exposed as ever a submarine could be, for it was impossible to dive with the fore hatch open. If surprised, we could do no more than defend ourselves with the gun or try an almost hopeless attack with torpedoes. We were no longer a submarine, in fact, but a cumbersome torpedo-boat with her engines stopped. No sub-mariner cares for such moments.

After what seemed an eternity, but what was timed by the stop-watch as three minutes flat, the report came through: 'Fore hatch shut and clipped.'

Thank God for that.

Then Paul Thirsk's voice: 'Course for position, two-seven-oh. May I start the echo-sounder, sir?'

'Yes, please, but don't transmit on the Asdic until I give the word. Group down, slow ahead together. Steer two-seven-oh.' Almost imperceptibly we gathered way.

We trimmed down, causing the entire pressure hull to sink below the water, and left only the bridge, gun platform and a foot of casing showing above the sea. Consequently we were invisible to the naked eye save at a range of well under a quarter of a mile.

Soon we were in position and I stopped the motors. After a final look round, the first folboat was launched, and Churchill climbed over the edge of the bridge. 'Remember', I said, as his face drew level with my own, *'you can see them, but they can't see you.'*

He muttered: 'Keep an eye on me', sat in the boat and started to paddle swiftly and silently towards the shore. He disappeared between two lights.

So far, so good. The night was still quiet save for the fishermen, and as I followed Churchill's progress through my glasses I was struck by the dreamlike atmosphere of it all. Surely this was far too peaceful and simple? There should be a dramatic appearance by the enemy, a pistol-firing chase, and a last-minute rescue. . . . My whimsey was cut short by the sight of Churchill paddling furiously back towards the *Unbroken*.

'What do you think it is, sir?' asked Haddow.

'Damned if I know', I replied.

Apprehensive and a little irritable, I waited until Churchill drew close, then climbed down to the casing to meet him. He was breathless from his exertions.

'What's up?'

'Naval patrols. There are several men in rowing boats. I'm sure they're naval. They hail each other.'

'Listen', I said, as evenly as I could manage. 'I've come nearly a thousand miles to do this job, and I'm not going to have the thing ruined by a few inoffensive fishermen. That's all they are. They only hail one another to help keep station and to let one another know of the catch. . . . Look.' I pointed. 'They're moving away slightly from your line of approach. You've a better chance now.'

'What will you do if they chase me?'

'I'll come and rescue you.'

'Would you use force?'

'They have no right to use force on you. If they try, we'll retaliate. We must smack it about. There's only just enough time to get through before dawn.'

I breathed a sigh of relief as he streaked back towards the shore. We saw him pass through a gap between the lights and he was then lost from sight.

'Tell our two braves their canoe will be at the door in half an hour's time, and tell the navigator to give them the money.'

'Aye, aye, sir', acknowledged the control-room.

We waited, restless. The strain was beginning to be felt now, for despite the apparent calm, we did not dare relax. The current had pulled us nearer the rocks that formed the crescent horns of the bay, and the acetylene lamps had

55

thinned out, suggesting that the fishermen were going to pack up for the night. So long as Churchill did not bump into them. . . . The gun's crew fidgeted. Still we waited. I sent Bill and the Ghost – the fourth spy whom I cannot remember – down into the folboat.

'Here he comes', said Haddow.

Paddling furiously, Churchill drew alongside. 'All's well', he greeted me.

'Your two lads are already in the folboat with their suitcases and money. . . . I'm going to turn the *Unbroken* round while you're ashore, so expect us to be facing seawards. Cheerio.'

With a quick wave the two folboats made for shore This time we would have to wait at least an hour.

'H.E.* bearing green nine-oh!'

God, what's this? A patrol?

'Probably a small diesel boat.'

It still might be a patrol. If it was we could only try to bluff them. 'Ask Jean to come to the bridge – and quickly.'

By this time the starboard look-out had also reported the ship. 'Now approaching from starboard beam', he added.

'Haddow! Get the gun on her.'

Through my glasses I could see that she was a motor fishing vessel showing no lights. She could be anything: smugglers, a naval auxiliary, or fishermen off for a black-market catch. Her course indicated that she had left Antibes harbour, north of the bay, and was heading for the open sea. She would pass fairly close under our stern. I heard from the casing the whispered reports: 'Trainer on!'; 'Gun-layer on!'; 'Gun ready.'

I said to Jean in French: 'Hail him and tell him to keep clear of us and the bay. Tell him we're on special patrol.'

Jean shouted across the water. His broad Breton accents added an authentic touch, for half the French Navy is recruited in Brittany. It was a knee-shaking moment, and it flashed through my mind that if she did not acknowledge

*Hydrophone effect from revolving propellers.

our hail within a very few seconds it would mean she was a naval craft and had not fallen for our bluff. I would have to open fire. But an answering shout quickly echoed across the water, and the trawler altered course away from us.

'Before this night's out one of us is going to have a heart attack', Haddow whispered.

As the trawler was lost to sight we went astern, turned round, and slid back into the bay stern first. When it was time to leave we could make a quick exit.

More agonised waiting. Cocoa was sent up for those on the bridge. The gun's crew were unlucky. Below, the air must have been thick and sour, for only those in the control-room were able to appreciate the freshness of the open conning-tower hatches. It needed the diesels to be running to suck fresh air through the boat.

'Do you think he's made it, sir?' asked Haddow.

I shrugged. 'God knows.'

It was quiet enough ashore, but that signified nothing. If Churchill had been apprehended, his captors would make no unnecessary sounds to put us on our guard. Instead they would notify Toulon and have fast pastrol vessels sent in search of us. *For how long can I leave the* Unbroken *exposed like this? How much time is Churchill worth balanced against the boat and its crew?* Questions without answers. I chewed my lip and wished to heaven we were far away to sea.

Finally Churchill loomed out of the dark, towing the empty folboat behind him.

'For God's sake snap into it, chum', said Haddow. 'Dawn's just around the corner.'

Churchill wasted no time, but took the remaining gear aboard his own folboat and was soon on his way back to the shore. While he was away the other folboat was hauled on to the casing and lashed down. Churchill returned within thirty minutes, and as he hove into sight, Taylor called from the casing: 'There are two men.'

For a fearful moment I thought he said: 'There's a woman', and envisaged terrible complications. But it was another man, right enough. There was no time to ask questions, however. Churchill's folboat was lashed to the other, the gun was secured, and everyone was sent below except the officer of the watch, the look-outs and myself. We moved out of the bay. As we gained distance from the shore the submarine was brought to full buoyancy. Again the gun was manned, the fore hatch was opened and the folboats disappeared below.

'Fore hatch shut and clipped.'

'Clear the casing. Fall out diving stations. Patrol routine.'

The operation was over.

South of Cap d'Antibes a lighted ship hove in sight. She was moving fast to the north-east and passed about two miles away from us – a Vichy destroyer. She was a little late.

In the ward-room Churchill introduced me to his 'guest' – a French ex-naval officer named Baron d'Astier de la Vigerie, but who went by the name of Bernard. He was one of the leading lights of the resistance movement. After we had shaken hands I told Churchill of the destroyer.

'One of the fishermen must have seen us and reported to the police. They, no doubt, telephoned Toulon. We were lucky, eh? A few minutes earlier. . . .' He broke off.

'Well, it was fun while it lasted', I said. 'Now I want some sleep. It's nearly light.'

Churchill smiled. Then, gravely: 'Thank you very much.'

'Don't mention it', I replied.

The next afternoon took us to the Bay of Agay where we were to land Jean and Léon. There was no precise spot where they had to be put ashore, and I chose a small beach between clusters of rocks. Up on the cliffs stood the Agay signalling station, but they could not see us, although the submarine was just visible from the shore at the point where Churchill landed his charges. The landing was a simpler duplication of the other. I closed to within two hundred and fifty yards of the shore, and the two spies paddled away with their wireless sets in one folboat, escorted by Churchill in the other. It was all over in twenty-minutes.

The game of cops and robbers ended, I had three days left in which to settle down to the business of sinking ships before the fuel-and-food problem forced us to start back towards Gib. Our Intelligence Service was rather scrappy about the Gulf of Genoa so I decided that the best thing to do was to creep to the south of the port and hope something would come out.

I sent for Thirsk and we pored over the charts. For'ard, Leading Telegraphist Johnny Crutch lost no time in sewing two daggers – symbols of two 'special' landings – on our otherwise virgin Jolly Roger.

3

APRIL 23RD.

At 11 a.m. we reached a position dominating the approaches to Genoa. It was a dramatic moment. At last we were in the 'free for all' area – that section of sea in which any vessel could be sunk on sight. For the first time since her launching, the *Unbroken* was patrolling the Mediterranean hungry for a kill. The order: 'Diving stations', and the report: 'All tubes ready', were no longer the parrot cries of just another exercise. This time we meant business.

The boat buzzed with excited chatter and wild speculation. Routine tasks were performed with revived zest and vigour, and even the motors seemed to purr with newfound sweetness. Naturally, I was pleased to see the crew in such good spirits, yet their enthusiasm afforded me a certain anxiety. For if an attack did come our way, it *had* to be successful. After all the months of waiting and training and anticipation, there would be a morale-shattering anticlimax if I failed them now. There was also the knowledge that as we were the only operational submarine in the Western Mediterranean, everyone at Malta and Gib. was hoping and praying for our safety and success. They were willing us their strength and their hearts, their prayers and their sinews, and I knew how much they hoped and expected of us. Such was our meagre shoe-string of resources, even the tiny *Unbroken* was a considerable weight in the balance of Mediterranean power.

It added up to a heavy and frightening burden of responsibility.

At eleven-fifteen we planed towards the surface, and as the water drained from the periscope glass I saw in the far distance the masts of numerous yachts and schooners. They made a charming sight against the green background of the Italian mainland – until one realised they were anti-submarine vessels. For a moment I was tempted to tackle one, but I knew we must concentrate on bigger game. Perhaps, if nothing else turned up, we would sink a schooner before making off. Such an action would undoubtedly close the port for a few days, for the Italians were more than a little sensitive of our submarines, and it would demonstrate that despite many misfortunes the Royal Navy still packed a punch.

So we bided our time and waited, slowly patrolling back and forth, with a constant and hopeful watch through the periscope. We ate hurriedly, and grabbed short spells of sleep, but the day and the night passed without incident. Disappointment stilled the chatter of the crew. Worried, I debated with myself whether or not to push off and hope for better luck on the way home.

And then, on the following day, towards the end of the afternoon watch, we drew a horse. An outsider, but a horse.

I was in the ward-room writing up the patrol report when Taylor's voice roared out: 'Captain in the control-room! Diving stations!'

Within three seconds I was at his side, and as I took the periscope from his hands he informed me: 'Smoke to the nor'-west.' There was a sudden prickling at the back of my neck. . . . Yes, there was smoke right enough. I altered course to intercept, and swung the periscope to sweep the rest of the sea and the sky. Both were empty. 'Group up!' I ordered. 'Full ahead together. Eighty feet.'

The hydroplanes tilted the boat to an acute angle and the

illuminated depth-gauge needles swung slowly round their dials. We shuddered as the propellers lashed us into greater speed. Down, down, down, in a rattling, rolling dive. . . . At eighty feet we straightened out. We were running blind towards our quarry – but were safe from prying aircraft. *Speed! Oh, for more speed!* I gripped hard the rungs of the control-room ladder and tapped my foot with impotent fury.

At our maximum underwater speed of about nine knots, it took us fifteen minutes to travel two miles, a distance a torpedo could cover in a fifth of the time. I ordered a return to periscope depth. 'Up periscope.' First the sky. Still empty. Then on to my target. A quick calculation told me she would pass across our bows in about twenty minutes – but at the impossible range of 12,000 yards. The chance of a hit at anything over 8,000 yards was infinitesimal. *We must get nearer.* 'Group up. Eighty feet. Full ahead together.'

Again we plunged downwards and forward. Fifteen minutes, each an eternity of waiting, ticked past. Thirsk, meanwhile, identified our target in Talbot Booth's book of silhouettes: a merchantman of 4,000 tons and some three hundred and fifty feet in length. Oh well, 4,000 tons were better than nothing. . . .

We crept up for a final look. The sea and sky remained empty save for our quarry wallowing along her unsuspecting way. I felt a moment of pity for her crew, doubtless sleeping off their vino and garlic lunch.

'Range now?'

'Seven thousand yards, sir.'

'Bearing?'

'Green one-five.'

The figures were fed into the 'fruit machine' operated by Haddow and Thirsk – an extraordinary contraption which, when given such information as the speed, bearing and range of the target, revealed just where and when a torpedo should be fired in order to score a hit. It was not infallible, depending as it did upon human estimations and calculations, but it was a help. On this occasion it told me we had two minutes to spare before she crossed our sights. I decided to creep nearer and reduce the range.

My heart raced and my mouth was dry.

From for'ard: 'Number One tube ready' . . . 'Number Two tube ready' . . . 'Number Three tube ready.'

From Cryer: 'Still a steady one-two-oh revs., sir.' Normally this would mean she was doing twelve knots, but I was certain that this cargo walloper had never done more than ten in her life, and was now crawling along at eight.

The D.A. – director angle – was set on the periscope by Chief E.R.A. Manuel, his arms around me holding the handles steady on the bearing as I watched the target creep into our narrow circle of view.

With infuriating slowness she approached the centre sight line.

Her range was so great that we would have to fire a dispersed salvo at forty-five second intervals – an unconscionable time to wait.

She was almost touching the sight line.

I swallowed.

'Stand by. . . . *Fire One!*'

The boat recoiled and bounced to the shock of the discharge, and a pressure on the ears indicated that the compressed air which fired the torpedo had been vented back into the boat. (The air had to come back into the submarine, for if it followed the torpedo into the sea, it would make an enormous white bubble.)

From for'ard: 'Number One tube fired.'

From Cryer: 'Torpedo running.'

Through the periscope I followed its track as it closed the distance between us and the merchantman. Despite its forty-five knots, the torpedo seemed to creep through the water like an aquatic snail. On . . . on . . . on, until Haddow, holding the stop-watch, ordered: 'Fire Two!'

Lord, was that forty-five seconds? It seemed as many minutes.

'Number Two tube fired.'

'Torpedo running.'

A quick glance at the cloudless and still empty blue sky, then on to the track of the second torpedo.

At last: 'Number Three tube fired.'

'Torpedo running.'

Now we could only hope. Savagely I gripped the periscope handles. 'We've *got* to hit her', I whispered. 'We've got to.' I straightened, gestured with a finger, and the periscope was lowered back into its well. 'Eighty feet. Group up. Full ahead together. Starboard twenty-five. Steer north.'

It was essential to get away from the tell-tale spot where the torpedo tracks started.

I stood at Haddow's side and watched the seconds tick past on the stop-watch. Everyone's ears were strained to catch the sound of a hit.

One minute.

Someone spoke but was immediately silenced. I raised my eyes and saw Churchill peering round the door of the ward-room. He winked. I winked back.

Two minutes.

We were a fair distance now from the torpedo tracks, so I ordered: 'Group down. Slow ahead together.' As speed was reduced the clattering vibrations diminished, and we would be able to hear more clearly the sounds of any explosions.

Six minutes.

I was soaked with perspiration and the air inside the submarine was a heavy foul blanket. To its natural staleness were added the odours of three dozen people who had neither bathed nor washed their clothes for a fortnight.

Seven minutes.

Still we waited. A heavy despair seized my heart. By this time the torpedoes had run 8,000 yards. Either we had missed the merchantman, or she was out of range. . . . Then we heard it – the unmistakable sound of a torpedo striking home, a noise Churchill described admirably as an outsize monkey-wrench falling on a corrugated iron roof. There was a great, spontaneous cheer from the sailors. Two minutes later we heard two deeper explosions as the other torpedoes hit the bottom.

Slowly we returned to periscope depth. The merchant-man was stopped and down by the stern. A plume of white steam trained upwards from her funnel. She listed badly to port. 'We've got her', I announced. 'Want a look, Number One?'

Quickly Taylor fixed his eye to the periscope. 'She seems to be sinking stern first', he said – and another cheer filled the boat.

There was no longer any point in loafing around at peri-scope depth. The water was clear and calm and a patrolling aircraft might well sweep across from the Italian mainland. We dived to eighty feet, 'fell out' diving stations, and headed seawards.

I felt I could claim the ship as 'hit, probably sunk'. She had a long way to go to the beach, and with Cryer's report that her propellers were stopped, a severe list to port and a hit in the stern, it did not seem a wild claim. My only fear was that no one would believe we had managed such a sinking at a range of over 8,000 yards. (There were, indeed, a few doubts about it among the sub-mariners at Gib., but they were quickly silenced when confirmation came through that the merchantman had gone down, Crutch, meanwhile, needed no confirmation before sewing a white bar on our Jolly Roger to signify the achievement.)

Steering southwards at eighty feet, we waited anxiously for retribution. Receiving a signal from the sinking mer-chantman, it was quite possible for a team of destroyers or patrol craft to be sent in search of us, backed up by low-flying aircraft. But none came, and I blessed our good fortune, and allowed myself to relax. I had forgotten the old Spanish proverb: 'Take what you want, says God, and pay for it.'

We had taken what we wanted, and were to pay for it

5

with the ugliest incident I had yet experienced in the submarine service.

We spent a further thirty-six hours in the Gulf of Genoa anxious to stalk fresh prey, but the enemy kept his distance and the time came to start back towards Gibraltar. Although disappointed, I reckoned that even if we had a clear run home our patrol had been justified. We were 'blooded' and I had proved myself to the crew.

In a way I was not sorry to pause for breath, for the intense concentration needed for the attack on the merchantman, coming after a long, debilitating period at sea, had left me tired and temporarily washed-out. But I was back on top of my form and impatient for further action when, at dawn on April 26th, soon after we dived, Thirsk called out: 'Diving stations! Captain in the control-room!'

Through the periscope I saw to starboard a schooner of some 200 tons. We were twelve miles off Bordighera, and still in the 'free for all' area. Hospital ships, boats carrying comforts to prisoners of war, and neutral vessels, would be some thirty miles to the south in the 'safe' area. Consequently I did not need to examine any books before deciding to attack her.

'Stand by gun action', I ordered – and again experienced a heart-thumping, throat-drying thrill of anticipation.

The gun's crew hurried into the control-room from for'ard and waited, curious, at the foot of the conning-tower.

'Open the lower lid, sir?' inquired Signalman Osborne.

'Yes, open up.'

He unclipped the lower hatch and the gun's crew, led by 'Pedro' Fenton, the gunlayer, climbed the conning-tower. As we surfaced he would open the upper hatch and lead the gun's crew to their action stations. It would be one of the rare occasions when a rating was first out of the conning-tower, and the reason was to save valuable seconds manning the gun. Haddow would follow them, timing his arrival to coincide with the firing of the first round so that he could start correcting the fall of shot immediately. Then it would be my turn.

'Bearing green three-oh, a schooner', I informed Haddow. 'Range oh-one-five. Open fire with H.E. on surfacing.' As Haddow passed this information to Fenton I turned to Taylor. 'Take her down to forty feet.' I lowered the periscope.

We started blowing the main ballast tanks at thirty-eight feet, held the boat down with the hydroplanes, reversed them and shot towards the surface like a cork.

'Up periscope.'

The schooner was steaming slowly on the same course. 'Deflection six left', I told Haddow, 'and remember the range is closing.'

'Aye, aye, sir.'

At twelve feet Taylor blew his whistle. As we made the last few feet to the surface the hatch flew open, the gun's crew scrambled out, and a flood of water poured down the conning-tower. I followed Haddow to the bridge just as the first shot was fired. The schooner was now some 1,500 yards away.

The first shell went to the left of her, the second over, the third I did not see, the fourth scored a hit – then the gun was silent.

'What's the matter?' I yelled.

'Breech jammed against round in the gun, sir.'

How the devil did they manage that? 'Open fire with Vickers.'

One of the two machine-guns on the bridge refused to fire at all. The other gave a feeble burst, coughed and was silent.

At that moment the schooner ran up a large new Italian flag. I caught my breath and tensed myself for unseen artillery to open fire on us. I had to act quickly.' Stand by numbers Three and Four tubes', I roared down the voice-pipe.

Powerless to do anything but wait for an Italian shell to scream past my ears, I muttered a brief, heartfelt prayer.

Then, from the voice-pipe: 'Numbers Three and Four tubes ready, sir.'

Thank God something's still working! The range was now no more than 800 yards. 'Starboard ten', I ordered. Our bows, two torpedoes ready in the nose, swung towards the schooner. As she was only crawling along I aimed my first 'kipper' just a fraction ahead of her bows. 'Fire Three.'

The boat rebounded, there was a burst of spray and the two-ton monster crashed into the water. To my disgust and horror its bubbling wake passed ahead of the schooner. She must have stopped just as we fired. I uttered a string of curses that would have done credit to a sergeant of Marines.

Incredibly, there was still no retaliation.

From the casing: 'Still can't clear the jam, sir.'

'Then clear the bloody casing.'

The gun was trained fore and aft and locked in position, and the gun's crew returned below. I leaned over the voice-pipe. 'Fire Four!'

There could be no mistake this time. The torpedo was aimed at the centre of a sitting target. I cleared the bridge and waited alone for the macabre, but fascinating, sight of a 200-ton schooner being blown to smithereens.

To my dismay, however, I saw no track racing through the water. The torpedo had disappeared! It was a nightmarish moment, and as I wondered whether I had gone mad there came the ear-rending roar of a thunderous explosion – *beneath our own bows*. Accompanied by a scorching blue flash that momentarily blinded me, it threw me against the side of the bridge and literally bounced the *Unbroken* out of the water. With a crash we slapped back into the sea, and as we righted ourselves there was a third plangent uproar below as equipment, crockery and machinery were hurled across the boat.

I climbed to my feet, still in one piece, but badly shaken. No serious damage could have been suffered below, either, or I would have been informed by now. Although dazed I could guess what had happened. The torpedo had refused to function after leaving the tube and had nose-dived towards the bottom until, at perhaps a hundred feet, the pressure of the water had actuated the firing mechanism.

I licked my lips and felt a chill run down my spine. *What the devil's the matter today? It's the 26th, not the 1st of April. . . .*

Back on an even keel we were again closing the schooner. There was still no sign of any retaliation and I reflected bitterly that they were saving their ammunition, content to watch us conveniently destroy ourselves. 'Enough is enough', I muttered, and crossed to the voice-pipe. There was little left for us to do, but I was damned if I was going to be seen off by a scruffy schooner. 'Stand by to ram!' I called. 'Stand by to board.'

At this point Haddow approached me carrying, not the Bible – as well he might – but a book listing vessels on the protected run. As we neared the schooner, the boarding-party ready in the conning-tower, I waited for at least a machine-gun to open fire in my direction. But we advanced in tense, uneasy silence. And then, as we drew close, we were able to discern the crew lining the deck – their hands above their heads!

'They've surrendered!' I cried. A moment later I could distinguish two minute flags flying from the schooner's masthead.

They were about the size of ladies' handkerchiefs – ladies' dirty handkerchiefs. 'Lord', I murmured, 'I think she's a P.O.W. comfort ship.'

By this time I could see her name, and as I read it out Haddow exclaimed: 'You're right, sir, she *is* a comfort ship.'

I felt a great wave of relief that I had not sunk a mercy vessel, but this emotion was soon replaced by black fury. I had wasted two torpedoes, had jammed my gun, had smashed a mass of equipment, had almost sunk myself, and had been made to look a blithering idiot – all because some cretin of a schooner captain could neither keep to a proper course nor fly a clean, decent-sized flag. I seethed.

'Stop both', I called down the voice-pipe. 'Fall out boarding-party.'

It was then another thought struck me – that it would never do for the schooner to report she had been fired upon by a British submarine. I remembered Peter Churchill was proud of his linguistic ability. Here, then, was a chance for him to air his Italian.

'Captain Churchill on the bridge!'

A minute later he scrambled through the conning-tower hatch. I handed him my megaphone. 'Ask them, in Italian, what the hell they think they're doing in this area. Then tell them to get to the south where they ought to be. Put it over as though you're the captain of this boat.'

As he bawled at them in Italian it struck me that Churchill made a convincing Wop U-boat skipper with his grey siren-suit, tanned skin and black curly beard, and I was reminded of the night in Antibes Bay when we had pretended to be Frenchmen. This bluff worked, too, and the schooner turned away to the south after making some pathetic excuse about being blown from their course by the wind.

In a better mood now, I ordered: 'Clear the bridge', adding to Haddow: 'Press the tit as you go down.' He did so, and the klaxon's stridence filled the submarine. I took a last look at the schooner, glanced round the sky to see if any aircraft were creeping in on us, saw the gun disappear beneath a white swirl of foam, and stepped into the conning-tower as the water gurgled up outside.

Down below I discovered that the damage we had suffered was quite superficial and had made more mess than mischief. None the less it was necessary to go through the tedious and unpleasant task of holding an inquest. Why had the gun jammed? Some fool had rammed home a shell without removing the base clip. Why had the Vickers misfired? They, too, had been loaded incorrectly. Why had the torpedo failed? It had not been checked to see that its

70

propeller was in the 'starting' position before it was hauled into the tube.

I decided against issuing individual punishments. Instead the entire ship's company would learn I had not been joking when I warned them at Barrow that only the best would satisfy me. They spent the entire dog-watches that day doing the severest exercises since the trials back in Scotland.

Later, in the ward-room, desperately tired and ready for sleep, I was greeted by a jittery Bernard and a slightly damaged Peter Churchill. It appeared the latter had been asleep when we tackled the schooner, and the first he knew of our encounter was when the wayward torpedo blew us out of the water. It also blew Churchill out of his bunk. For a moment the poor chap didn't know whether we were still afloat or plunging to our deaths. To add to his confusion he was struck on the head by a flying electric toaster and a pair of dividers stabbed him in the knee. Badly shaken, he sheltered beneath the ward-room table with Bernard wondering what the dickens it was all about, until I summoned him to the bridge. Hearing of this, my admiration for Churchill increased tenfold, for he had given no indication of the nerve-destroying shock he had suffered when he gallantly hectored the skipper of the schooner.

Next morning yet another incident was added to our chapter of accidents. We dived at dawn, as was our custom, but it took us over ten minutes to get down. The reason, without becoming too technical, was that the water kept in the submarine to help us dive had been pumped out during the night. Fortunately, during the period our tail was stuck in the air no enemy aircraft paid a visit, but I was not in the mood to let the matter pass lightly. Taylor, as first lieutenant, was responsible for our diving trim and irrespective of who actually made the error, it was Taylor who got it in the neck. I was reluctant to give him a bottle – it in no way improved our relationship – but the slip-up might well have cost us our lives.

*

During the final leg of the journey to Gib., I finished my last letter to Ting. I had written several on patrol and would post them in a batch on return to harbour. Needless to say, my thoughts were always with Ting in her Aldeburgh cottage. I would visualise her dancing with the pongos on Saturday nights at the Brudenell Hotel, or walking along the front in her green slacks and brightly coloured jerseys. Aldeburgh was such a small, quiet, quaint old town it never crossed my mind it was a target for bombing and machine-gun attacks; that it was in a perpetual state of alarm as the point where the enemy bombers crossed the coast for their raids on London; that it was 'windy corner' for night actions in the North Sea against German 'E'-boats. I am glad I did not know these things at the time. It was better to think of Ting and our child safe in a charming and isolated seaside resort – and never once did she write a word to disillusion me.

I wondered what June looked like, whether she would be beautiful, whether she would be jealous when I came home – if I came home. I wondered what the little cottage was like inside, and would picture myself there with them. I wondered if the pongos stationed near-by were making a pass at Ting and decided they all were. It made me feel rather proud, but not jealous – I knew my Ting. . . .

On May 2nd, exactly three weeks after leaving Gibraltar, we sailed into Algeciras Bay, the crew lining the casing and the Jolly Roger fluttering above our heads. Entering harbour after a patrol is a moving experience, for mingled with the pride of the occasion comes the shock of realising you might never have come back at all; might never again have seen these well-remembered landmarks and heard the familiar voices of friends. One patrol or a dozen, this feeling of surprise would still be there.

We secured alongside the *Maidstone* and I went aboard her to report to Captain Voelcker. My legs were stiff and unresponsive as I climbed the depôt ship's ladder, the result of lack of exercise and cramped living, and my thighs and shins were aching by the time I entered the 'cuddy' – the Captain's cabin. Thinking of the misfortunes listed in my patrol report I presented myself to 'S' with mixed feelings, but he soon put me at my ease with a cheery: 'Glad to see you back. Have a sherry.'

I did.

'We've had early information about the spies you landed', Voelcker continued. 'All four of them are doing well. More than that Intelligence won't say, but it's enough to show that you did your part of the job satisfactorily.'

As Voelcker was congratulating me on our kill in the Gulf of Genoa we were joined by Peter Churchill and Bernard. The news of Bernard's presence had already been grape-vined round Gib., however, and in no time at all a couple of Army Intelligence officers came to whisk him away for interrogation. The party broke up and I made for my cabin and a much-needed bath. An hour later, resplendent in monkey jacket, bow tie and crisp linen, I took up a strategic position by the ward-room bar. I was able to relax with a free mind. The crew had been fixed with leave at the local rest camp, our list of defects had been handed in, and the patrol report was written. Our misfortunes were best forgotten. For a couple of days, at least, I could take it easy.

To my delight, I was joined at the bar by three old friends, all sub-mariners. There was Harry Winter, who had served with me on the China Station and had recently brought the *Unbending* from England; Edward Stanley, who had come out to be spare Submarine Commanding Officer in case any operational skipper fell sick; and David Ingram, captain of the *Clyde*, who was spending his days running petrol and other supplies to Malta.

From Winter and Stanley I heard news from home. It was still a picture of gloom. No more white bread, fuel rationing to be introduced, an offence to waste paper. Beer, whisky and tobacco had all increased in price – if you could get them – and the *Luftwaffe* continued to bombard our

73

cities. The R.A.F. were hitting back, but the B.B.C. announced with depressing regularity such dasasters as the sinking of the cruisers *Edinburgh, Dorsetshire* and *Cornwall,* and the aircraft carrier *Hermes,* and Japanese gains in the Far East.

Then Ingram told us of the position at Malta – a grim, defiant story of sinkings, near starvation and empty cartridge-cases.

Inevitably we reminisced, and the gloom disappeared. The party ended with a riotous game of hockey in the cabin flats and an unskilled attempt at furniture removing. The next morning found me with a woolly head and the need to account for an overturned wardrobe.

Our stay at Gib. was beset by numerous petty irritations. During our patrol Laval's pro-German government had taken over in France, and there was a strong likelihood that French capital ships and cruisers stationed at Casablanca would attempt to break through the Straits to join the rest of their fleet at Toulon. If they did it would be our duty to sink them. The watch on leave had to be recalled from the rest camp, and we spent a tense week ready for sea at a moment's notice. Fortunately, the scare died down, but was immediately replaced by a different one – the threat of saboteurs.

The danger of sabotage by frogmen based on hostile Spain had become very real, and our nights were constantly disturbed by motor launches chugging round the harbour dropping miniature depth charges on suspected intruders. Our own sentry was warned to 'fire first and ask questions later' – an order that nearly led to the deaths of certain members of the Gib. army garrison.

A group of them decided to 'capture' the *Maidstone* via the submarines tied alongside, and our sentry's dreams of home were interrupted one night by the appearance of two swimmers clambering over our bows. He drew his revolver, but some sixth sense stayed his hand. Instead of firing he challenged them, and they promptly 'surrendered'. In no time at all they found themselves under guard aboard the *Maidstone*, very lucky to be alive.

When the frogman scare had died down it was found that one of our main batteries had become contaminated with oil from a leaky fuel tank and needed to be replaced. This was a major job of work and entailed removing part of the casing, lifting a cover plate from the pressure hull, and then hoisting out one hundred and twelve cells, each weighing a quarter of a ton. Then, new cells fitted, and the heavy connections strapped down, everything had to be replaced. It was a laborious lengthy job which kept the crew hard at work just when they needed – and deserved – a rest.

At this time a personal problem came to a head. I could not get away from the fact that Taylor and myself had certain incompatibilities of temperament. Such differences might pass unnoticed in a big ship, but they are exaggerated and distorted in the emotional confinement of a small submarine. Taylor, I decided, must be replaced. It was no reflection on him as a man or as a sailor. It was simply that our temperaments did not allow us to serve together. As there were no spare first lieutenants aboard the *Maidstone*, I asked Haig Haddow to take the job. It was an embarrassing moment for both of us, but he said, simply: 'Yes, sir. Can do.' Next came the unpleasant business of going to 'S' and asking that Taylor be relieved. Captain Voelcker did his best to dissuade me, but I was firm and insisted that it would be him or me. I took a risk there, for 'S' might well have said: 'Very well, it'll be you.' After all, Edward Stanley was aboard the *Maidstone* spending his time trying to break a C.O.'s leg so that he could take his place at sea! in the end, however, 'S' gave way and John Haig Haddow took over. (It is only proper to add that Taylor went to another submarine, won his own command, and served with distinction.)

Lieutenant 'Ted' Archdale, R.N., a very fair, very precise twenty-year-old from Northern Ireland, came as armament officer, and we were also given the luxury of a 'spare' officer – 'Tiger' Fenton, R.N., a dark, thin and wiry lieutenant from Oxford, also just twenty years old.

This time a great wad of mail had been awaiting us at Gib., and I spent a nostalgic hour catching up with news of Ting. She had taken a cottage at Aldeburgh, and both she and June were fighting fit. Excitement entered her life when Vickers invited her to Barrow to launch a new submarine, the P.48. She was delighted to accept, of course. Not only did they pay her fare and hotel bill, but rolled out a red plush carpet from the station to a waiting Rolls-Royce, and treated her as if she were visiting Royalty. Escorted to the launching by the commander of the cruiser, *Jamaica*, she smacked a bottle of Empire wine across the bows of the P.48, then put a further, moderate supply of the stuff to an even more exhilarating use! It appeared that a good time was had by all.

In my reply I commented on the luxurious life she was leading, and warned her to expect a visit from a certain Peter Churchill. I added that any uncomplimentary remarks concerning his misadventures aboard the *Unbroken* were to be taken with a pinch of salt.

Another week passed before Intelligence finally 'released' Churchill, and we had made our good-byes after a merry and lengthy farewell party. I was sorry to see him go, for I had grown to like him a lot during the three weeks we had spent together.

Our troubles and breakdowns put in order, we were able to enjoy ourselves once more. There was plenty of bathing, picnicking and swimming, and the officers could go sailing at the Yacht Club – remembering to keep clear of the Wrens, most of whom still examined the number of rings on your arm before examining the regularity of your profile. The boat's hockey and soccer teams did their stuff, and sustained more casualties on the murderous gravel grounds than the enemy were to inflict. It was all very jolly and amiable, until a month had passed and boredom crept in. None of us were sorry when the news came through that we were off to sea again.

By this time we had been joined by two 'S' class submarines, including the *Safari* commanded by the legendary Ben Bryant and the *Unison* commanded by Lieutenant A. C. Halliday. When the *Unbroken*, *Unison*, *United* and *Unbending* went to Malta to rebuild the 10th flotilla, the 'S' boats were to help form a new 8th flotilla based on Gib.

Four of us were to take part in this next operation; the protection of a Malta convoy from Italian surface forces. An enemy cruiser squadron was known to be based in the Tyrrhenian Sea, and the four submarines were to take up a patrol line between Cagliari, the Italian naval base in southern Sardinia, and Palermo in Sicily. *Unbroken* was given the billet nearest the Sicilian coast, but as the four of us had to cover a line one hundred and eighty miles long, the chances of intercepting an enemy force were not great.

How we cried out for more submarines! But there were none. Rumour had it that the Americans had been asked to send boats to the Med., but had declined saying their submarines were too large to operate in those clear, restricted waters. True or false, it made us feel extremely proud.

Before sailing we lost another member of the crew. The hapless rating who had been responsible for jamming the gun was found to be suffering from nervous strain – 'bomb-happy' was the more popular way of putting it – and had to be invalided back to England. Then, with him safely ashore, I had a final glass of sherry with Captain Voelcker and sailed east towards the sunrise.

4

JUNE 12TH.

At 5 a.m. we dived near Marittimo Island off the north-west coast of Sicily and proceeded to our station north of Cape St Vito between Trapani and Palermo.

All that day and most of the next passed without incident, and while the crew were conscious now of the folly of reck-less speculation, they were soberly aware of the desperate need for our mission to succeed. This was not merely a case of trying to sink an enemy ship for the sake of an extra bar on our Jolly Roger: the fate of Malta and the Med. – and thus, perhaps, the war – might well depend upon the arrival or non-arrival of the convoy from England. Hungry now for both guns and bread, Malta could not survive for ever on mere fist-shaking gestures of defiance.

At this point the convoy would be nearing the Skerki Channel before passing between Cape Bon and Marittimo. As we had not been informed of its precise movements, or of the size and deployment of its escorting force, we did not know exactly when they would enter the Sicilian Channel. My calculations told me that for a period on June 15th, between leaving their Gibraltar escorts and linking up with aircraft from Malta, the merchantmen would be nakedly alone, presenting the Italian cruisers with a perfect target. I could only guess where this gap would occur, as

V.A.C.N.A.'s* staff at Gib., for reasons best known to themselves, had kept us in ignorance of the overall plans for the operation. All the *Unbroken* could do was remain in position off Cape St Vito until the enemy cruisers were sighted or reported.

Soon after we surfaced on the night of the 13th we received a signal from *Safari*. She had sighted the cruiser force which had left Cagliari and was steaming in our direction. I read the signal and climbed to the bridge, grinning happily. A cruiser force – and all ours! I altered course to intercept.

Just before midnight *Unison* sent me another enemy report, and by plotting the two I reckoned the cruisers were heading for Marittimo. I adjusted my own course towards the island.

Hopes ran high when the darkened lighthouses on the Sicilian coast started to flash, suggesting the enemy was about to pass our way and needed the lights to aid navigation.

At one-thirty we saw searchlights and bursting ack-ack fire over distant Trapani. Our circraft from Malta were doing their stuff.

As we peered into the moonless and starless night, hardly daring to breathe, straining to catch the slightest hint of throbbing engines or crashing bow-waves, the thrill of the situation captured our imaginations. At two o'clock, however, the wind was taken from our sails. In the wireless office Petty Officer Willey intercepted a reconnaissance aircraft's report to Malta – the cruisers were over a hundred miles to the north-east of us and steaming east. Since leaving Cagliari they had made considerable alterations of course at speeds which put us right out of the picture with our surface maximum of less than twelve knots. It transpired they had passed near enough to *Unison* for her to fire a salvo – a following long shot that had little chance and did, alas, miss.

*Vice-Admiral Commanding North Atlantic Station.

We dived at dawn as a fresh outbreak of ack-ack fire punctured the Trapani sky. Too weary now to be aware of our frustration and disappointment, we slept while we could and kept a permanent watch at periscope depth. But the day passed uneventfully, and we surfaced at dusk wishing we had something more practical than prayers to offer for the convoy's safety.

Soon after midnight we received a signal from V.A.C.N.A. at Gib. The ever-alert aircraft from Malta had spotted the cruisers leaving Palermo three hours previously. Our hearts leapt at the news, for we were only seventy miles from the port and good fortune might bring the enemy our way. We closed Marittimo again, assuming the warships must pass there if they were making for the convoy.

An hour later Cryer reported: 'Heavy H.E. bearing oh-seven-oh; distant; moving right.' The cruisers, right enough. But they were ten miles off and legging it away from us. Once again we had been cheated of a target.

Bitter at our inability to do more than limp slowly after the rapidly disappearing cruisers, we pressed forward as best we were able. We dived at dawn, and at eleven o'clock we heard it – the crashing of bombs and the bursting of shells as the cruisers, backed by aircraft, commenced their attack upon the convoy. We did not realise it then, but four merchantmen were sent to the bottom. For seven hours our ears were tortured by the sounds of the convoy's anguish, and through the periscope we saw the black smoke of death hanging over the horizon some fifty miles to the south. Malta's hopes, and the hopes of the Allies, were fading fast beneath the brilliant sky. In the morning a convoy had been sailing to relieve beleaguered Malta. As dusk gathered only a pathetic handful of wreckage floated on the oil- and blood-stained sea.

That evening we sighted the foretops and mainmasts of two of the cruisers as they returned from their victory, but they were ten miles off and inside Marittimo. Again they had dodged us, and two months were to pass before we finally caught up with them. . . .

I was upset at my inability to plot the enemy's movements which caused me to lose a fine target. As I commented in my patrol report: 'It is to be noted that in my attempt to appreciate the course of action of this enemy cruiser force, I was seriously handicapped by my complete lack of information regarding the positions and movements of our own convoy and naval forces. I submit such information should be supplied in future as it is disheartening to feel the enemy probably has more knowledge of this subject than oneself.'

The Admiral at Gibraltar agreed with this sentiment.

On the morning of June 17th, awaiting further orders from V.A.C.N.A., we dived at 4.30 and I decided to grab a few hours' sleep. I had not been long turned in when I was awakened by the familiar: 'Captain in the control-room!'

I found myself there half-asleep. I noticed we were below periscope depth and still diving. Thirsk, the officer of the watch, explained. 'A Cant seaplane, sir, searching the area. Dawn patrol, perhaps. I'm going down to seventy feet. She's some way to starboard at the moment, but she's been milling around all over the place.'

The mention of the Cant soon woke me up. Designed for anti-submarine work, and with such a low speed they could almost hover like helicopters, they were a flaming nuisance. I gave this one a quarter of an hour in which to clear off, then crept back to periscope depth. (The art of such a manoeuvre is to glide gently upwards using no extra speed, in order to avoid disturbing the even pattern of the smooth sea. Then, if your tormentor is still around, you can slip down again before he spots you. At forty feet I raised the attack periscope. There is always a fascination about peering through a periscope, even for the thousandth time. At first you see nothing but the clear blue water thirty feet above your head. As you rise the light broadens until, with a crystal flash, the periscope bursts through the surface and

6

you are gazing at the world above the sea.

On this occasion, however, the romance was shattered, for as the periscope broke surface I found myself looking straight at a very large, very horny and very rusty mine! It floated high on the surface only fifty yards from my eye – and we were heading straight for it. No, not quite straight. The thing would pass down our port side – but only just.

I swallowed, but said nothing. There was, indeed, nothing to say or do. The mine was so close to us that any disturbance might detonate it. I hoped it was a simple contact mine and not acoustic or magnetic as well. It was not barnacled and had therefore been laid fairly recently, and although its top was wet, the sea was not splashing over it, suggesting it had only just broken from its mooring. I thanked God it had not freed itself a minute later. . . .

As though hypnotised, I watched the brute as it receded past the port beam. I switched the periscope to the sky. The Cant had gone. I sighted back on to the mine and beckoned to Thirsk. 'If you want a whiff of reality', I said, 'take a peek at that.'

He did so and gave an odd smile.

With a wave of my hand I returned to the ward-room.

Three hours later V.A.C.N.A. came through by wireless and ordered our immediate return to Gib.

There were few smiling faces awaiting us at Gib. God knows they had little about which to smile. Four of our best and fastest supply ships and tankers had been wiped out, and although a handful of fighters had got through – flown from the escort carrier before she turned back to Gib. – they were useless without fuel. Four minesweepers and six M.L.s got in but could do little without fighters.

Malta was really in a bad way. The ships of Force K – the destroyers and cruisers based on Malta which had inflicted such magnificent damage on the enemy in late 1941 – had been sunk or disbanded. Its last cruiser, *Penelope* – 'The Pepper Pot' – had struggled into Gib. badly damaged long since. None the less, Malta fought on. Apart from anything else, she had diverted a thousand German bombers from the Russian front at a time when the *Luftwaffe* needed them at Stalingrad. But now, at the end of June, 1942, it looked as though the George Cross Island had shot her last bolt. Rommel was romping towards Alex, with the most highly mechanised army in the world. While his supply lines were measured in hundreds of miles, those of the Eighth Army stretched for thirteen thousand.

This, and more, was explained by 'S' at a conference aboard the *Maidstone*. Present were the C.O.'s of the other submarines at Gib.

'We *must* get to Malta', Captain Voelcker said. 'The only way to save the Eighth Army and give them time to build for a counter-attack is to cut off Rommel's supplies. There is no way of achieving this save by operating from Malta. There are two obstacles: getting there through the mine-fields and the sound chance of being bombed to hell on arrival. Overcoming the first obstacle depends upon good fortune. The second can be overcome by spending the days submerged on the bottom of Valetta harbour and surfacing only at night. Unpleasant, but expedient.' He broke off and surveyed the gathering. 'Mars.'

I jumped. 'Sir?'

'I've decided that you will have the privilege of leading the new 10th flotilla back to Malta. It won't be easy getting there and it won't be a picnic when you arrive. But I feel you can cope. Later you will be followed by the *Unison*, *Unbending* and *United*.'

There was nothing to say but: 'Thank you.'

The *Unbroken* was docked for a quick scrape and paint. It was impossible to guess when the next opportunity for an overhaul would occur, for all the dry docks at Malta had been bombed out of existence. Coat after coat of anti-fouling composition was applied, our cracked and worn paint was sand-papered down, the rusty patches were burnished and covered with preservative, and we finished the job with four coats of deep blue paint. I could imagine what the crew were thinking by the time they started on the fourth coat – *Fighting's supposed to be our line, not pansying-up for some bloody inspection* – but there was method in my thoroughness. Blue was the colur of the sea, and blue would be the colour of the *Unbroken*. I intended that we would stay blue, for in the clear waters of the Med. red rust patches were easily spotted from the air.

While the sailors painted and the *Maidstone*'s technicians gave us a thorough overhaul, I spent a great deal of time with David Ingram who had made many trips to Malta through the minefields with the *Clyde*. There was no such thing as following her route, for her track varied with each journey. Underwater navigation is a tricky business. You cannot keep to a set, marked course as though you were driving a car along Piccadilly. To keep only to within a mile of your prescribed route while submerged and blind is not as irresponsible as it sounds, for your slow cigar of a submarine is greatly at the mercy of unknown underwater currents and tides. In any case, even if one could keep to a few yards of a former route, a deviation of inches might involve hitting a mine. So despite Ingram's experience and valuable advice I was going to be very much on my own.

There was no doubt concerning the density of the mine-fields, for the Germans and Italians had used E-boats, aircraft and U-boats to mine every possible approach to Malta. The island was a night's jaunt from Augusta in Sicily, and as the enemy believed you could not mine a section of sea too heavily, hardly a night passed without new ones being laid. In certain waters it is possible to sail beneath a minefield, but the approaches of Malta, and Valetta in particular were too shallow to permit such a simple way out of the problem. *Clyde* had run her supplies to a point on the island's south coast, and the particular hazards of Valetta were unknown. The last submarine to sail from there was the *Olympus*, commanded by Lieut.-Commander H. G.

Dymott. She was bringing from Malta the commanders and crews of the P.36 and P.39, both of which had been sunk by bombing, and she struck a mine outside the harbour. Although surfaced at the time, only five of the hundred-and-twenty men aboard the *Olympus* managed to swim back to harbour. The rest were lost.

In the interests of security, the crew were told they were preparing for an ordinary patrol, but the cat was out of the bag when our kit was brought aboard from the *Maidstone*, and we stocked up with engineering and electrical spares. I lectured the crew on the need for secrecy, and I'm glad to say my lecture was heeded. Secrecy was kept – until two cases of Scotch were sent from Government House boldly inscribed, for all the world to see: 'LORD GORT, MALTA'!

For the officers at Malta we loaded gin and sherry, while the sailors at the base there – H.M.S. *Talbot* – were remembered by the inclusion of three tons of dehydrated vegetables.

Stuffed with extra gear and food, some had to be stowed in the ward-room. Our tiny living-space, already over-crowded by the presence of Tiger Fenton, was a shambles, much to the chagrin of our 'flunkey', Able Seaman Butterworth. The war had cruelly interrupted this young man's career as a student of economics, and when he arrived at Barrow he was detailed off as 'ward-room hand' to the annoyance of both himself and the numerous volunteers who saw in the job an opportunity to nobble the ward-room gin. Young Butterworth – he was barely twenty – brightened our lives considerably, although not always intentionally. Tall and slender, with aristocratic features, I sent him to our digs at Barrow to give Ting a hand with the housework during her pregnancy. He proved himself most cheerful and kind, and his farewell to Ting is firm in her memory: 'You know, Mrs Mars, I'd much rather stay here with you than go to sea with your husband.'

For all his innocence, and the inevitable raggings it produced, he was a hard worker and one of the few sailors who never missed a patrol.

Seeing the chaotic state of the ward-room, Haig Haddow sent for Butterworth. 'Look at this bunch of bananas', he fumed. 'What the devil do you think the Captain's going to say when he comes down? Butterworth? Did you say your name was Butterworth? Butterworthless is more like it.'

'Sir! You can't speak to me like that', came the indignant reply. 'I am a gentleman with two banking accounts.'

'Good God', said Haddow, 'I never knew!'

Before leaving Gib. I had a final look on the charts at QBB 255 – the name given to the main enemy minefield. It lay, a vast, rectangular threat blocking the Sicilian Straits, bounded by a line drawn from Marittimo across the Cape Bon, from there down the Tunisian coast to Ras Mahmur near Hammamet, then across to Pantellaria and up to Cape St Marco on the south coast of Sicily. Since enemy convoys used it, the area was not entirely mined, but it was a tough enough spot just the same.

I spent our last night at Gib. sitting on a balcony of the Rock Hotel watching, perhaps for the last time, the setting of the sun over the distant Atlantic. I felt very relaxed and calm, and strangely confident of success – despite the pessimistic implication of the letter in my pocket. When we had first arrived at Gib. I considered the possibility of getting killed and decided I ought to make some provision for Ting and June. The answer seemed to be an insurance policy. Not a large one – just a thousand pounds for Ting in the event of my non-return. In my pocket was the insurance company's reply. Yes, they would willingly insure me, but the premium for a thousand pounds was five hundred smackers a year! Since my pay was less than five hundred a year I decided I could not afford to get killed even if a convenient opportunity presented itself!

*

86

The following afternoon we waved farewell to the *Maidstone* and sailed eastwards to pour a tiny drop of lubricating oil on Mr Churchill's rather rusty 'Hinge of Fate'.

Our journey passed quietly until 4 a.m. on July 18th when we dived to eighty feet south of Marittimo for the passage through QBB 255. I decided on a direct, bold route, suspended half-way between bottom and surface, that would take us straight through the minefield via Cape Granitola. The distance of the run was sixty miles – fifteen hours of it at four knots.

The thought of QBB 255 gave us all the jitters. The sense of helplessness. . . . The fact that you cannot hit back but are permanently on the defensive, listening, waiting, magnifying every jolt and movement. . . . You speak in whispers as though loudness of voice will, in some indeterminable way, add to the hazards, and you are reluctant to make any but the most necessary gestures or movements. It is nerve-racking business.

Inside the minefield I had the mine-detecting unit – a refinement of the Asdic – switched on in an effort to plot the pattern of the mines and sail between them. A regrettable action. We plotted mines, right enough – ahead, to starboard, to port, above, below – everywhere! Cryer's eyes popped from his head as he reported each new echo, and a few wild expressions and quivering lips were to be seen in the control-room. I found it difficult to overcome a tremendous temptation to alter course as the mines were reported, but common sense prevailed and we continued dead ahead. A submarine going through a minefield can be compared to a man walking through line upon line of soldiers with a ladder on his shoulder and his eyes shut. As he passes through one line he *may* hit a man in the line in front, but if he swings round he is *certain* to hit, not one, but half a dozen. So we kept to the straight and narrow.

Slowly, blindly, we crept forward, while the air thickened and our sweat-soaked clothes clung to our bodies, until, unable to bear any longer Cryer's maddening and demoralising reports, I ordered: 'Switch that bloody thing off and never switch it on again!'

The hours dragged past in uneasy, clock-ticking silence. We lapsed into a half-sleeping state of stiff-jointed, head-throbbing weariness, and it came as a shock to realise that it was nine o'clock – we were through the minefield, and could surface.

Surface we did, and fresh air never smelled sweeter. I altered course to starboard for the sixty-mile run that would take us to our final hazard – the mine-blocked channel into Valetta.

We dived at the entrance of the channel as the new day opened a reluctant, bloodshot eye over the eastern horizon. The channel was sixteen miles long, shaped, roughly, in a semicircle, only half a mile wide at its broadest point, and beset by strong currents and tidal streams. To add to our difficulties, the big periscope was jammed in low power, and we could not obtain long-range fixes of position from the Malta coastline. As our orders were to surface at sunset one mile from the Castile Signal Station, we pressed on and hoped God was still with us.

After the exhausting fifteen hours in QBB 255 I was devoid of emotion towards this second minefield, and my mind was assailed with other, sadder, thoughts – memories of friends and messmates of yesterday whose shattered bodies lay but a few fathoms below our hull. It is said that mourning is selfish – that you weep, not for the dead, but for your own loss. That may well be true, and my memories were a shroud of grief, for I had lost many good friends and noble companions among these tortured waters. . . .

It was the end of a beautifully calm summer's day as we turned ninety degrees to port towards Grand Harbour. The periscope revealed a sky untroubled by cloud and waters unrippled by breeze.

'Diving stations! Stand by to surface', I ordered.

'Check main vents', said Haddow.

'All main vents checked shut, sir.'

Haddow turned to me with a smile. 'Ready to surface, sir.'

'Very good. . . . Thirsk. Time of sunset, please.'

'Seven-forty-six, sir. Two minutes to go.'

'What's the private signal?'

'T-A-G, sir.'

I nodded my thanks. '*Unser Tag.*' How appropriate.

I told Osborne to take a look through the periscope at the Castile Signal Station. 'Got it?'

'Yes, sir.'

'Right. Follow me up and give the private signal without delay.'

'Aye, aye, sir.'

Once again the boat was alive with movement and chatter. It was more than a reaction to the minefields – it was an awareness of the fact that we were starting on the greatest of our adventures together.

'We're in position, sir,' Thirsk reported. 'I make it sunset.'

'Surface!'

Osborne opened the lower lid, allowed me to climb to the top of the conning-tower, then followed armed with the six-inch Aldis lamp. As we broke surface I opened the upper hatch, was soaked with water and was greeted by the sound of a bugle call from the fort. I stood aside as Osborne beamed the Aldis towards the signal station. At once they replied.

'Recognition acknowledged, sir.'

'Group up. Half ahead together. Start the engines.'

Fifteen minutes later we nosed towards the Lazaretto on the shore of Manoel Island. A voice called across the water. 'Here you are! Number two billet, between these buoys!' I recognised Lieut.-Commander Hubert Marsham waving from the foreshore. I waved back.

We were soon moored bow and stern to the buoys and a

pontoon was run out to connect us with the shore.

A minute later I was saluting Marsham and shaking hands with Lieut.-Commander Giddings, the First Lieutenant of the base. He was second in command to Marsham who had taken charge in the absence of 'Shrimp' Simpson.

Marsham led me to the ward-room. 'I expect you'd like a gin.'

'You bet', I replied.

'I feel I owe you one', he continued. 'You've no idea how glad I am to see you.'

I smiled. 'You may rest assured of this, my dear sir. You're not nearly as glad to see me as I am to see you!'

Understandably, the sailors lost no time making their presence felt in and around Valetta. Although beer was rationed to one bottle per man per week, many ratings had 'bottled their tots' during the voyage from Gib., and were well stocked with good, strong naval rum. The practice of bottling one's tot was quite illegal, and officially it did not happen, but I would be interested to hear of an alternative explanation for the uncertain footsteps of the watch ashore as they staggered across the pontoon to the island. My own attitude towards the matter was quite simple: with all the uncertainty of tomorrow at sea, let them enjoy themselves today on shore so long as they do not get into any serious trouble. As it happened, our first night at Malta produced only one 'casualty' – Able Seaman Jeff McTeare from Carlisle. Touring Valetta with his pal, Micky Jones, he was picked up by the patrol in the Colonade and run in because of his 'excessive high-spiritedness'. When Micky, with Irish perversity, insisted on accompanying his oppo, the patrol willingly obliged.

Next morning the padre, visiting the cells, came to McTeare and inquired solemnly: 'And why are you here, eh?'

McTeare raised his heavy throbbing head and replied in a hollow voice: 'Because the bloody door's shut.'

I heard of this incident later, for the padre, good chap, did not report it, and when McTeare was sent to me for punishment, I did my duty by awarding him no more than ten days' 'Number Eleven' – a sentence that involved ten day's extra work during his off-duty hours, and loss of rum. (On reflection I must admit that at no time during my command of the *Unbroken* did I ever see such punishments enforced, but I am not certain whether that was due to my lack of observation or the kind-heartedness of my first lieutenants!)

After the first novelty of Valetta, however, very few of the crew bothered to cross to the town from Manoel Island. Apart from one or two doubtful cafés, Valetta had little to offer save rubble and air raids.

The inevitable nightly raid, now accepted as an essential part of the islander's lives, shattered the peace of our arrival. It followed a pattern familiar to most people in Britain – bombs, shells and tracers filling the night and the ears with monstrous noise and fire, then the unreality of the quiet that followed the All Clear. The raids on Malta differed from those at home in two respects: their greater frequency, and the fact that they left few fires burning, for there was little to burn on the island's rugged sandstone.

It was arranged that while one watch and an officer stayed aboard at night to deal with possible emergencies, the remainder would sleep in the comparative safety of the air-raid shelters of the Lazaretto, an old hospital-cum-storeroom dating back to the Knights of Malta. The officers were permitted to sleep 'upstairs', but were instructed to make for the shelters if the raids were 'Sixty Plus' – if sixty or more aircraft were in the attack. The men ashore in Valetta were told to take cover if things became really nasty.

The morning after our arrival, having weighed-off McTeare, I wondered how best to defend the *Unbroken* against daylight air attack. I was reluctant to implement Captain Voelcker's suggestion that we should dive by day, and puzzled my brains for an alternative scheme. In the end 'Jan' Cryer produced a bright idea – camouflage. Haddow brought the suggestion to me with great enthusiasm. 'There's a solitary tree on shore,' he elaborated, 'and if we lop off its branches we can break the boat's outline.'

It seemed sound enough and was given my approval. By the time the job was finished, however, the tree on shore was little more than a stump, and the *Unbroken* a shapeless mass of twigs and greenery. It was then that Thirsk pointed out, with great diffidence, that as there wasn't another bush or tree in sight for miles around, he had never seen anything that looked so obviously like a camouflaged submarine. He was right, of course. The branches were ditched overboard, and an hour later the problem was solved for us by 'a higher authority'. It had been decided that when a raid was on its way a system of smoke-screens would be touched off, and both Grand Harbour and Lazaretto Creek hidden in a cloud of white smoke. The enemy could drop his bombs, but he would not be able to pick out individual targets.

After twenty-four hours at Malta we were joined by the *United* commanded by Tom Barlow. We got together to congratulate one another on coming through in one piece and to share a general hate against QBB 255. Later that night Captain Simpson flew in with a skeleton staff of three officers, and at dawn next day four minesweepers started a sweep which blew seventy mines from our inward route!

I was anxious to get to sea on patrol before enemy bombers sank us in harbour, as they had sunk other submarines before us, but there was nothing doing. I kept pestering the Staff Officer, Bob Tanner, until he said, rather pompously I thought: 'Don't chase the war, young Mars. The war will catch you up.'

How right he was!

Finally I learned the cause of the delay. We were to take part in OPERATION PEDESTAL, the defence of the now famous August convoy to Malta.

On July 30th we sailed, our orders scribbled by Captain Simpson on a signal-pad, but comprehensive for all their brevity. We edged down the channel escorted by fighters, and preceded by the minesweeper *Rye* – a pleasing change to our method of arrival.

Our patrol was to start off Naples and then to work down the Calabrian coast until we found a suitable spot to gun the main railway to the south. To thoroughly wreck the railway would be as good as sinking a large merchantman, for it was so heavily used it was estimated that for every twenty-four hours it was out of action Rommel lost 14,000 tons of supplies. After the bombardment we were to take up station near Messina with at least four torpedoes remaining to protect the convoy against any cruiser force that might loom up. The whole operation would take about eighteen days.

The minesweeper turned for home, and we experienced again the nerve-fraying miseries of QBB 255. We survived it and surfaced at dusk, and I took up my position in my newly designed 'bedroom' – the bridge. To save time in the event of action I'd had a specially constructed steel deck-chair lashed to the bridge. The two ends of the canvas seat and back were made with pockets that fitted over the chair's framework. Thus, if there was some flap I would leap to my feet, grab the canvas and throw it down the conning-tower, all in one movement. Its 'smack' against the deck of the control-room would serve as the first indication that something was afoot. Unfortunately there were to be occasions when I rushed below forgetting the canvas, and Morgan, the second coxswain, was kept occupied manufacturing new ones.

Two incidents marked the next seven days – both unsuccessful attacks on enemy merchantmen. They cost me four torpedoes and I experienced the same nagging uncertainty I had known in the Gulf of Genoa – the fear of the effect of these failures upon the crew. They were working hard and risking their lives, and when it came to the great moment it appeared as though I let them down. The situation was such that one of three things had to follow – success and a new lease of life, a watery grave, or my being relieved by a new C.O. As far as I was concerned, only one of those three alternatives was at all satisfactory.

5

THE *Unbroken* was the first of the 'U'-class submarines to be
fitted with a 3-inch gun. Former boats had been equipped
with 12-pounders, toys of little use against anything bigger
than a rowing boat. Because of this, train-wrecking had been
a hazardous, cloak-and-dagger affair carried out by intrepid
gentlemen operating from folboats. Outstanding among
them was the army's Captain 'Tug' Wilson who did
magnificently courageous work paddling ashore from submarines and laying explosive charges along the lines.

Ours, however, was to be a more elaborate and snappier
job.

During the afternoon of August 8th we examined the
shore between Paola and Longobardi through the high-
power periscope; a short stretch of coast high on Italy's
instep along which the electric track was in full view. After
a conference in the ward-room I decided to do my strafing
at a point a mile north of Longobardi. It held many ad-
vantages, including the useful landmark of Mount Cocuzzo,
an absence of civilian houses, and deep water inshore.

After sunset, as the dusk melted into night, we steered to
within three-and-a-half miles of the coast. At 9 p.m. we
surfaced and crept towards land at four knots, propelled by
our near-silent motors. Fifteen hundred yards from shore
we stopped – and waited.

The next hour passed in dark gentle silence. The night

was black and starless, relieved only by the red and green railway signals and tiny pin-points of light sneaking through the curtains of the Longobardi cottages. With luck we would soon be giving the inhabitants a new item of conversation with which to enliven their small-town gossip. . . . I stretched my arms and turned my face into the soft, off-shore breeze. There was only the slightest of swells to give any feeling of movement, and the look-outs saw nothing around them but dark, empty sea. Below, the crew were at diving stations. It would be a hot, sticky night for them, for there was little ventilation without the engines running, and the boat was already an oven after a day submerged. In the control-room Thirsk studied his charts and checked them against the echo-sounding. The area was well mapped and we were able to determine our gun range to within fifty yards. The gun's crew were huddled on the casing, their feet but a few inches from the water, the first round of flashless night ammunition ready in the breech.

One grave fear was uppermost in our minds – that our target might be blacked-out and we would have to fire blind at the distant sound of its electric motors. If that were the case, our charts giving us the range only to within the nearest fifty yards, we could fire a hundred rounds without doing an iota of damage. I could, of course, fire a star shell, but that would reveal our presence to every sentry, aircraft and ship within a radius of thirty miles. The problem caused me a great deal of concern until, at ten-ten, a train came into view heralded – to our joy – by a large headlamp. Its seemingly disembodied beam moved mysteriously through the night, and we were able to obtain an accurate, last-inch, range from it. A few minutes later an up-train passed – assuming they did travel 'up' to Rome – and at ten-forty our own bundle of fun came into sight. She, too, was adorned with a great lamp.

We had moved to within 900 yards of the shore, and at a whispered order the gun's crew closed up. Archdale leaned across the bridge. 'Range a thousand yards, deflection

96

twenty right. Independent firing. Open fire when she reaches the datum point.'

'Aye, aye, sir.'

There was a long pause as the gun held the train in its sights until it reached the datum point.

Ten-forty-six.

With a roar the gun opened fire, its tiny spurt of crimson swallowed quickly in the darkness. The shell screamed through the air and exploded with a tremendous crash.

A hit, by God!

Indeed it was. There was a vivid blue flash as the overhead wires were brought down and in its brilliance I saw the engine detach itself from the coaches and idle on down the track. Again the gun roared, and again. After five rounds, all of them hits, the carriages and trucks crackling merrily with dancing yellow fires. The signal lights were out – the power was off. Archdale transferred his attention to the engine and methodically blew it to pieces.

By 10.48 it was all over. With cold-blooded ease we had deprived Rommel of at least twenty-four hours of supplies – 14,000 tons' worth. It had been achieved in precisely two minutes at a cost to ourselves of ten rounds of 3-inch ammunition. I was elated with the brilliant shooting of Fenton and Co., for it was an extraordinary feat, performed with the smooth, effortless ease of a not too difficult gunnery exercise. But congratulations would have to come later, for it was essential to get out of the area and start south towards our rendezvous near Stromboli.

Half an hour later I saw the train still ablaze in the distance. It was a reassurance that I had not dreamed it all.

Our daylight patrol position for PEDESTAL was two miles north of Cape Milazzo lighthouse which lay eighteen miles west of the Messina naval base. It was not a comfortable spot, for the enemy were certain to have the area bristling with every anti-submarine device they could muster. I had said as much at Malta, but it was pointed out that the

7

Admiralty at Whitehall were organising the convoy operation, and it was they who had chosen my position. I felt the Admiralty should have confined themselves to giving the route of the convoy, and should have left the business of choosing covering positions for the submarines to on-the-spot authorities at Malta, but I thought it as well to say no more than: 'It's a bit close.'

At 12.15 on the morning of August 10th, at about the same time as the convoy was passing through the Straits of Gibraltar a thousand miles to westward, we reached a point four miles from our position, and took a look round. Visibility was good, the sea was calm, only a slight breeze blew from the north-east. Owing to a combination of minor faults and bad sea conditions, the Asdic was out of action. But the hydrophones, which picked up audible sounds as distinct from the supersonic noises picked up on the Asdic, were working, and we had not long been there when the report came up the voice-pipe: 'Mushy H.E. bearing one-eight-five.'

Puzzled, I went below and listened. Through the earphones I could hear a soft tapping; a sound quite unlike any I knew. It seemed to come straight from Cape Milazzo. It was constant, its bearing did not change, and the disturbing thought struck me that we had been picked up by some new-fangled detection device. I said nothing, however, but waited until dawn, when we dived and closed towards our patrol position.

Still the soft, monotonous tapping.

At 9 a.m., four miles north-west of Milazzo lighthouse Thirsk summoned me to the control-room. 'Ship coming towards us from the direction of the Cape, sir.'

I grasped the handles of the periscope and looked. An enemy patrol tug coming straight towards us. As there was no harbour or anchorage under the lighthouse it suggested she was being 'beamed' on to us. I thought at once of the mysterious tappings and did not like the situation one bit.

'Eighty feet. Starboard twenty-five.'

Down we plunged, and the next fifteen minutes passed in uneasy silence. And then, just as I was deciding it had been a false alarm, there was a *krrump,* and the boat shuddered to the explosion of a depth charge. From experience I assessed it at being some four hundred yards off – as were the four others that followed. We promptly went into 'silent routine' which meant that in order not to transmit noises for the enemy to pick up, all machinery, such as ventilation, refrigeration and water circulation systems were shut off, leaving only the motors and gyro-compass running.

I glanced around the control-room. Apart from the licking of lips and the wrinkling of foreheads, the others gave no indication of the tense anxiety they must certainly have been feeling. I experienced the same combination of nerves, claustrophobia and fury that I had suffered when sneaking through the minefield for, as on that occasion, we were essentially on the defensive, powerless to hit back, unable to run away – simply wallowing there waiting for the enemy's accuracy of fire to improve.

But no more depth charges followed the first pattern of five and after a while we crept back to periscope depth. The patrol tug was about a mile away – steering back towards the Cape. All very peculiar.

We returned to our patrol position, and for an hour nothing happened. At 11.15, however, smoke was sighted – a *Cretone*-class minelayer steaming towards us from the Straits of Messina, escorted by a Cant flying-boat. The hydrophones were still picking up that extraordinary tapping, which seemed to confirm that the enemy was beamed on to us.

We went to a hundred and twenty feet, and half an hour later depth-charging commenced.

For an hour it went on: patterns of four or five, with an interval of perhaps ten minutes between each pattern. Oddly – and fortunately – they were seldom closer than within three hundred yards of the *Unbroken* – far outside their lethal range. As a result, we were disturbed by nothing more than heart-jumping *krrumps* and occasional shudders – but all the time there was the nerve-fraying fear that the next one might hit the bull's-eye, and the *Unbroken* would be the subject of another solemn 'Admiralty regrets' announcement. At 1.15 our tormentor was joined by a pal, and the two of them continued the bombardment. We kept to our irregular zigzag, and while I cursed the infernal device that had beamed the tugs on to us, I blessed its lack of absolute accuracy.

My clothes were soaked in sweat, the air in the boat was thick and oily, and my nerves were in a wretched state. If only we had been able to hit back! If only there had been some movement or action to take our minds from the agony of the situation! But no. We could only wait and hope and pray, brooding and exaggerating, picturing a torn, smashed hull and a bubbling, choking, lung-bursting death. . . .

Then, at three o'clock, they moved away. The tension eased. I 'fell out' diving stations and told Leading Stoker Fall that he could pass round tea and sandwiches. I was tempted to sneak back to periscope depth for a look round, but reason prevailed and we lumbered along as before – course, oh-three-oh, speed one-seven-five revs., depth a hundred and twenty feet.

It was getting on for 6.30 before the enemy made the next move.

That was when Cryer reported 'H.E. to starboard!' and before the words were fully out of his mouth a pattern of charges dropped close enough to shake the rivets from our plates.

I felt sick in the stomach. It was approaching dusk, and we simply had to surface before midnight in order to re-charge our batteries and replenish our air. If we failed to do this we would be able to survive for no more than a further twelve hours. . . .

We've got to get out of here!

After the first teeth-rattling pattern the enemy reverted to his curious behaviour of bombarding the sea a quarter of a mile away from us, and I took advantage of the fact to slip into the ward-room to study the charts and plot my next move. We were half-way between Cape Milazzo and Stromboli, having steered roughly north in our attempt to dodge the depth charges. Apart from the fact that the position ordered by the Admiralty was a 'natural' for underwater suicide, it was obvious that the enemy, knowing of our presence, would not send his cruisers into the Cape Milazzo area. I decided to choose another position, although it would be impossible to inform 'Shrimp' Simpson at Malta of the change. One pip on the W/T and the ever-watchful enemy would be able to fix our position to within the nearest hundred yards. For an hour, to the disturbing background music of distant *krrumps*, I made a careful appreciation of the inland sea between Malta and Gibraltar. In the end I decided on a position half-way between the islands of Stromboli and Salina, reasoning that it was the best point of interception if the cruisers were using the port of Messina. It puts us thirty miles from our ordered position and if it turned out to be a miscalculation, I was well aware of the fact that I'd be hung from the highest yard-arm in Whitehall 'as a mystery and a sign' – probably with a cowardice charge thrown in for good measure.

At 7.15 the enemy pushed off, and I assumed that as good Italians they were more concerned with going home to embrace their mistresses than with sinking a British submarine. On the strength of this assumption I told Joe Sizer, the cox'n, to issue tins of tongue for a cold supper.

Paul Thirsk did a little simple arithmetic and informed me that exactly seventy depth charges had been hurled in the general direction of the *Unbroken* that day.

At 10.30, fifteen miles from Milazzo, I decided to surface. It was a tricky, yet necessary, decision, for the enemy might well have returned to the area and could be waiting with stopped engines for the *Unbroken* to refill her lungs.

Quietly we went to diving stations and crept up to eighty feet.

We listened. All was silent.

Sixty feet. Still silence.

Periscope depth. I stared intently into the big periscope. The night was so dark that only a solitary star confirmed that the periscope was actually out of the water. The horizon was indistinct, and a careful sweep did not reveal even the suggestion of a shadow to mar the evenness of the night.

I handed the periscope to Thirsk and told Haddow to plane the boat to the surface and blow number Four main ballast tank with low-pressure air when we reached twelve feet. In this way we would surface slowly and in silence. As the conning-tower broke from the water I leapt to the bridge followed by Archdale and Osborne. Quickly we swept sky and sea through binoculars. Nothing in sight. I reckoned that if we were unable to see the enemy – if he was there – then he couldn't see us, either.

With the faint glow of Stromboli's volcano to port, I ordered: 'Half buoyancy. Group up. Half ahead together. Start the engines.'

Let's get out of here!

Shortly before dawn we dived fifteen miles north-west of Stromboli, and looked forward to a quiet, lazy day catching up on lost sleep. Having made certain a thorough periscope watch was being kept, I turned in and managed to grab four hour's rest. This was double the stretch I usually enjoyed, and gives some indication of my exhaustion after the strain of the depth-chargings. I had trained myself to sleep with my ears open, as it were, and any sounds, such as alterations to course, immediately wakened me. Apart from these interruptions, it was a standing order that I should be given a shake by the officer coming off watch every two hours in order to know exactly what had been happening – if anything. But on this occasion I slept for an undisturbed four hours – until 12.30 p.m. when we reached the 'Mars Patrol Position' twelve-and-a-half miles west-south-west of Stromboli peak.

The rest of that and the following day were quiet for us – but not for the convoy. As I was to learn later, it had been cruelly savaged.

All fourteen merchant ships were modern and fast, capable of at least fourteen knots. All were of desperate importance to Malta. Accompanying them was one of the most powerful escorts in history. There were the battleships *Rodney* and *Nelson*, the aircraft carriers *Illustrious*, *Victorious*, *Furious*, *Eagle* and *Indomitable*, the cruisers *Manchester*, *Nigeria*, *Cairo* and *Kenya*, no less than twenty-five destroyers, while six submarines patrolled off enemy ports.

On Sunday, August 9th, the convoy sailed through the Straits of Gibraltar fully aware that casualties were going to be heavy, but quietly confident that the convoy would get through. It did – at a price.

On Tuesday the *Eagle* was hit by four U-boat torpedoes, rolled over and sank. After flying-off thirty-eight Spitfires which reached Malta and gave cover to the convoy later on, the *Furious* returned to Gib. escorted by five of the destroyers. Luckily, a salvo of torpedoes aimed at the *Nelson* missed, but the *Indomitable* was hit by three bombs, the destroyer *Foresight* was torpedoed and sunk, the *Nigeria* was torpedoed and had to return to Gib., the *Cairo* was torpedoed and had to be sunk. The grim slaughter went on. On Wednesday, the heavy covering forces returned to Gib. as per plan, for the enemy control of the air was too powerful even for the remaining three carriers. Two merchantmen blew up on Wednesday evening, and the *Kenya* limped along as best she could after being struck by a torpedo. Wave after wave of bombers, E-boats and U-boats tore into the convoy. Four more merchantmen were sent to the bottom, and the *Manchester* was torpedoed – or struck a mine – and had to be scuttled.

The Royal and Merchant Navies suffered terrible punishment in those forty-eight hours, but they won their fight. On the evening of Thursday, August 13th, 1942, three ships sailed into Valetta, and Malta was saved. The following morning two more limped in, including the tanker *Ohio*.

But we knew nothing of this as we watched and waited off Stromboli, and spent Wednesday night baking in a midnight temperature of eighty-eight degrees. I was asleep in my deck-chair when Tiger Fenton tapped my shoulder. 'Captain, sir! The P.O.Tel. has a signal in the control-room. It's emergency.'

Automatically, as I crossed the bridge, I noted the absence of moon, the dull glow of Stromboli, the flat calm of the sea and the part-clouded sky.

Below, Petty Officer John Willey handed me the pink slip. From Vice-Admiral Commanding at Malta, it read: 'Enemy cruisers coming your way.'

My heart sank and I could have groaned aloud, for 'your way' referred to Cape Milazzo, thirty miles to the south. As I wondered what on earth I should do, an explanatory signal came from 'Shrimp'. At 3 a.m. an aircraft had reported enemy cruisers off Sicily's Cape de Gallo steering east at twenty knots. This meant that they would pass my original position off Cape Milazzo at 7.30 a.m. – in two-and-a-half hours' time.

My immediate reaction was to order a full-speed return towards Cape Milazzo. I could get half-way there by dawn. And the enemy, making a detour around the area of the depth-charging in case we were still there, might well fall into our hands.

I lighted a cigarette and had another look at the charts. As I did so I was struck by a second possibility. The enemy Admiral would know he had been reported because the aircraft which spotted him would have been bound to have dropped a flare. That being so I reckoned he would have the good sense to alter course at least twenty degrees. Since he could not alter to starboard because of land, he would have to alter to port – and into our welcoming arms!

I could see no other alternatives and made a decision which, as far as Lieutenant Mars was concerned, was momentous. We would stay where we were.

We dived early and I altered the breakfast-hour to seven o'clock on the time-honoured principle of food before battle. In the middle of my bacon and eggs, assailed by doubts as to the wisdom of my decision, I heard Cryer report to the officer of the watch: 'H.E. ahead, sir.'

That was all I needed. With a bound that sent my breakfast crashing to the deck I was in the control-room and holding the big periscope in my hands.

'Diving stations!'

The crew knew what was afoot and hurried eagerly to their positions.

'H.E. bearing two-three-oh . . . Heavy units . . . Fast.'

I swung the periscope. The morning was fine but for a distant haze hanging over the surface of the sea. I could see nothing from the direction from which the H.E. was coming. I took the earphones and could hear a confused jumble of noise. It certainly came from heavy ships, but they were a long way off. I went back to the periscope.

My heart thumped like a trip-hammer, but I noticed with satisfaction that my hands were steady and my eyes were clear.

Then I saw them as their masts broke through the haze on the horizon. In my joy I could have danced a jig.

'Bearing now?'

'Green one.'

They were now well over the horizon. 'Two . . . Three . . . Four! Yes, four cruisers in line ahead, coming straight towards . . . Range?'

Chief E.R.A. Manuel read off from the range scale above my head. 'Range, twelve thousand, sir.'

'Down periscope. Port twenty-five. Group up . . . Up after periscope.'

As the smaller periscope cut the surface I had a quick look round for aircraft close to. There were none; but two anti-submarine Cants hovered over the cruisers.

'Down after periscope. Fifty feet.'

Fifty feet would have to do. I wanted to keep my eye on

this magnificent array of ships, and it would take too long to get down to eighty feet and back.

As the needles passed thirty-five feet I ordered: 'Full ahead together.' I turned to Haddow. 'Two 8-inch cruisers and, I think, two 6-inch. Anyhow, four cruisers for certain.'

Haddow raised an eyebrow. I nodded. He passed the glad tidings over the broadcaster in a commendably calm quiet voice.

Archdale was manipulating the fruit machine, knowing it was my intention to get into a position whereby, as the cruisers passed, I would have the entire lengths of their sides at which to aim. 'Course for a ninety-degree track, sir, one-four-oh.'

'Steer one-four-oh.'

The helmsman eased his wheel. The planesman levelled up.

'Course, sir, one-four-oh.'

From Sizer: 'Depth, sir, fifty feet.'

We shuddered as the propellers lashed the water and the submarine leapt across the enemy's bows at her top speed. Assuming the cruisers kept to their course we would have to get some eight hundred yards off their path, turn around and fire. I had fifteen minutes in which to do this – just time enough.

I then announced an item of information I had kept to myself. 'There are eight modern destroyers and two seaplanes escorting. Shut off for depth-charging.'

As Haddow relayed the information to the rest of the boat, I felt a moment of queasiness. It was a feeling I knew of old – a boyhood memory of a twelve-stone brute flashing down the touchline of a rugger field, the full back at the other side of the field, and only myself to bring him down. . . .

This time, however, I was not alone. I looked at the faces around me.

Haddow, an enigmatic smile on his lips, watched the depth gauges like a lynx. On him depended whether I would be able to see or not when the moment of firing came. Thirsk was crouched low over his chart, oblivious to everything save the job in hand. Archdale gazed oddly at the fruit machine as though it was about to give birth. On him depended the director angle. Cryer, humped over the now repaired Asdic, had a grin on his face I can only describe as fiendish. E.R.A. Lewis hovered by the telemotor and blowing panels, watching the pressure indicators with deep concentration. Manuel stood behind me ready to read off the periscope and keep me clamped to the director angle at the time of firing. The planesmen, communicating numbers and helmsmen sat with their backs to me, working their controls with practised ease.

Throughout the boat it was the same. Men going about their duties calmly, intelligently and efficiently, well aware that this was a 'now or never' opportunity – a torpedo attack against heavily escorted units travelling at high speed. There would be no second chance. We had to deliver a single, swift knock-out punch.

'Bring all tubes to the ready', I ordered. 'Torpedo depth settings fourteen and sixteen feet.'

After a run of three minutes we crept it back to periscope depth. I lifted my finger and the attack periscope was raised until the eyepiece was just clear of the deck. I curled into a squatting position and looked. Still under water. Lewis raised the periscope, slowly dragging my body up with it. As soon as the top glass cut the surface I whisked around to see if anything was too close to us. Then on to the target.

'Down after, up for'ard periscope.'

The line of cruisers had altered course to starboard – away from the direction in which we were heading – and had taken up a form of quarter-line. This meant the nearest would be one of the 8-inch cruisers. She would be my target. Although the range was rather more than one could wish, the disadvantage was cancelled by the fact that the new formation presented an excellent multiple target – one of the more distant 6-inch cruisers might be hit by a torpedo that missed the 8-inch job. I congratulated myself on this stroke of luck, and turned to study the eight evil-looking destroyers and their accompanying aircraft – the boys who could well wreck my chances.

Fortunately five of the destroyers were well out of it on the far side of the cruisers. Obligingly, the aircraft had gone that way, too. The aircraft might come back, but I reckoned I was safe at periscope depth for the time being. The other three destroyers were still in line ahead, and if they did not alter course I would be able to sneak across their bows and fire from inside the 'screen' – from between them and the cruisers.

'Down periscope.'

Archdale looked round. 'New enemy course, oh-seven-oh. What speed shall I allow, sir?'

Thirsk said: 'Speed from plot twenty-two knots.'

Cryer reported: 'Two hundred revs., sir. That gives twenty-five knots according to the table for Italian 8-inch cruisers.'

'Give them twenty-five knots', I said. Archdale manipulated the fruit machine.

'Director angle, green three-six-and-a-half.'

Thirty-six-and-a-half degrees. That was the amount I would have to 'lay off' from the direction in which our bows were pointing. A big angle. It would need care.

'All tubes ready, sir. Torpedoes set at fourteen and sixteen feet.'

'Very good.' Torpedoes set at that depth, hitting a ship doing twenty-five knots, would make as big a mess as anyone could wish for. I glanced at my watch. Exactly eight o'clock. *They'll be having breakfast now, or getting ready for a run ashore at Messina. They'll be lucky!*

I felt good. In my pint-sized submarine I was going to tackle twelve enemy warships all at one time. A story for my grandchildren – if the destroyers and aircraft let me live to tell it!

'Slow together . . . Stop starboard. Up periscope.'

The tip of the attack periscope nosed out of the water. I grasped hard the handles as though to stop it protruding too far, and raised my little finger when six inches were exposed. Lewis stopped it dead. I swept round quickly to fix the covering aircraft. They were still over the other side of the 'screen'.

From Archdale: 'Target bearing green five-oh.'

'How much longer to go?'

'Three-and-a-half minutes, sir.'

The three destroyers in line ahead were still tearing towards me, although I was just a fraction inside them. With luck I would have a clear view of my target. They could not have picked us up on their Asdics or they would be circling ready to drop depth charges, but they were going to pass us too damn near for comfort. I could go deep and fire by Asdic, but I was reluctant to do this as firing at a noise is obviously less accurate than firing at a seen object. None the less, we set the Asdic angle, just in case.

All this flashed through my mind in less than a second, and a moment later I uttered a loud curse as I saw the nearest destroyer alter course straight towards us. She was no more than fifteen hundred yards off. I did some quick thinking.

'How much do *Navigatori*-class destroyers draw?'

'Fifteen to eighteen feet, sir.'

It meant she would pass over our hull but not over the conning-tower. Unless she missed us by the narrowest of margins, her keel would snap off the periscope and slice our conning-tower with the ease of a tin-opener. It was a risk we would have to take. I had no intention of losing my target.

Our target. . . . I swung the periscope. There she was, still on the same course. To my joy I saw that overlapping her was one of the 6-inch cruisers. I had a double length at which to aim.

I winced as I swung back to the destroyers. The crashing

bow-wave of the nearest was less than a thousand yards off. A little voice nagged at the back of my brain: *Remember your command course training. A fast destroyer, head on at about a thousand yards. Go deep! Go deep, you bloody fool! You haven't a hope.* . . . 'Down periscope.'

Archdale said: 'Just under a minute now, sir.'

'Stand by all tubes. . . . Lewis, if my periscope is knocked off as the destroyer passes over, put up the for'ard periscope without further orders. Understand?'

'Very good, sir.'

'Director angle green three-six-and-a-half', Archdale reported.

'Asdic bearing of target green four-two.'

'Up periscope. Bearing now? Range now?'

'Green three-nine. Range three thousand.'

I swung the periscope. Two destroyers had passed fairly close. The third towered above me. I felt very calm. I could see the stem cutting the water like a monster scythe. . . . The for'ard gun . . . A part of the bridge. She was too close for me to see more, but I was a hair's breadth off her port bow and unless she altered course she would not ram us. With a deafening roar she rushed past, and I caught a momentary glimpse of a scruffy-looking sailor smoking a 'bine as he leaned against a depth-charge thrower.

Manuel's breath was hot on my neck as he strained to keep me clamped to the director angle. As the destroyer's stern flicked past my nose, the target came on my sights.

'Fire One!'

The boat jumped with the percussion.

'Half ahead together. Down periscope.'

'Fire two!' Archdale gave the order from his stopwatch. The fast target allowed for an interval of only eight seconds between torpedoes.

'Fire Three!'

From Cryer: 'One . . . Two . . . Three torpedoes running.'

'Eighty feet! Group up!'
'Fire Four!'
'Hard a-starboard. Full ahead together.'
'Fourth torpedo running, sir.'
We spiralled downwards. . . .

6

On a south-westerly course eighty feet deep we hurried from the firing position at a rattling nine knots.

I was very aware that the passing destroyer had caused me to fire late and I hoped the speed of my target had been over-estimated.

The seconds crawled past.

The scene in the control-room might have been transplanted from a militant Madame Tussaud's – the tense, still figures, some standing, some sitting, others crouching, all rigidly silent, unblinking and tight-lipped, straining to catch the sound of a torpedo striking home. For two minutes and fifteen seconds we were like that, until a great clattering explosion brought a back-slapping roar of triumph to shatter the illusion.

We've done it! We've hit the cruiser!

Then, fifteen seconds later, a second explosion.

'Tell the boys it's two hits for certain!'

What a moment that was! Fused into one mighty brain and body, the 600-ton *Unbroken* had tackled four cruisers, a couple of aircraft, and eight submarine-killing destroyers. Had tackled them and beaten them. Were we capable of lyric poetry we'd have composed a Psalm of Thanks, for we felt as boastful and as proud as David must have felt that afternoon in the valley of Elah.

We did not have long to glory in our success, however.

Four minutes after firing there were other, more sinister explosions – the familiar *krrumps* of distant depth charges. In a flurry and a panic the destroyers were hurling 'ashcans' – depth charges – in a somewhat belated defence of the cruisers.

Then Cryer reported: 'Asdic transmissions bearing green one-four-oh, sir.' The enemy had pulled himself together and was after us. This was soon confirmed by a pattern not far beyond our stern.

'One-hundred-and-twenty feet. Group down. Slow ahead together.'

A minute later we were at a hundred-and-twenty feet, sliding along at less than three knots.

'Silent routine.'

The ventilation and cooling systems were stopped, as was every piece of machinery in the boat save the compass and the slowly revolving main motors. Orders were passed in whispers, all unnecessary lighting was doused. The Italians were not as efficient as our own side in the use of Asdics, but they were hot stuff picking up things on their hydrophones.

There were at least three destroyers after us, sweeping in to drop depth charges at the rate of one a minute. The patterns were closer than anything we had experienced before, their nearness judged by two sounds apart from the violence of the vibrations.

One was the sound of 'rain'. This occurred after an explosion and was caused by gushers of water – often many tons in weight – falling back into the sea. You have seen pictures taken from the surface of depth charges exploding – how the water is forced into the air like the blowing of a gargantuan whale. This water crashes back into the sea like heavy rain, and when you can hear it in a submarine it's pretty close to you. The second noise was a sharp, metallic *click* which preceded the explosions by perhaps half a second. It came from the firing mechanism and to be able to hear it meant, again, that it must be too close for comfort.

In the next forty-five minutes each of our tormentors

8

performed eight or nine runs culminating in patterns of five or seven charges. Many were close enough to bring down the insulating cork from the hull, but I soon came to the conclusion that the enemy had no idea of our depth. The firing was accurate, but the charges were set to explode shallow, and we were out of real danger so long as we kept at a hundred-and-twenty feet.

By nine o'clock, after 105 depth charges had been dropped, it appeared the enemy had either lost us or had gone off for further supplies of depth charges. Had we possessed any more torpedoes it would have been our duty – and pleasure! – to return to the scene of the attack to finish off a lame duck or kipper one of the destroyers. But with our 3-inch gun we would have had as much chance against an 8-inch cruiser as a puppy with a pea-shooter against a rogue elephant. A cruiser is a different proposition from a railway train!

We had no means of knowing whether the enemy had left a destroyer behind to track us at dead-slow speed while the other returned for depth charges, and after our experience off Cape Milazzo we did not under-estimate the Italian's ability to stick to us once he'd truly found us. Therefore, although all was quiet above us, and no more ashcans came our way, we kept to silent routine until dusk, grabbing a snack meal of cold meat and tea towards noon.

In a way, the *thought* of a depth charge attack is worse than the attack itself. Once an attack has started there is little to do but wait, sweat and pray, a process less of a strain on the nerves than the fear that there *might* be a ship stalking you, there *might* be an aircraft circling overhead, there *might* be a sudden fury of explosives about your ears. So it was, from nine in the morning until seven at night, we endured ten unbroken hours of silent misery, hardly daring to breathe, talk, or move our cramped limbs.

At seven o'clock we planed to periscope depth.

Nothing in sight. Two hours later we surfaced and sent a

report to Malta of the morning's encounter. 'Shrimp' Simpson ordered our return.

Next day we received a heart-stirring message from Malta. Air reconnaissance reported that we had hit two cruisers with our one salvo – an all-time record which, so far as I know, stands to this day. I did not think it improper to order an extra tot of rum all round. I felt we deserved it.

Years later I was able to piece together the story of this cruiser squadron. In August, 1942, Italy was badly short of fighter aircraft, and the Germans had promised to provide the air cover for the cruisers' attack on the Malta convoy. The Italians set out but the aircraft did not arrive, and their Admiral, on Mussolini's orders, promptly turned tail for home. On the way we caught him – and serve him right!

The 8-inch cruiser we torpedoed was the *Bolzano*, and although there was only one casualty, the torpedo hit deep in an oil fuel tank and set it on fire. The fire gutted the ship and she had to be beached. Towed to Naples and then to Spezia, she was finally attacked by frog-men and scuttled.

The 6-inch cruiser, *Muzio Attendolo*, had sixty feet of her bows shot off and limped into Messina. Patched up, she was taken to Naples for more thorough repair work. There she was bombed by the Americans and became a total loss.

It is therefore a fair claim to say that we destroyed two cruisers with our one salvo of torpedoes. As it turned out, severely damaging them was more effective than sinking them, for they tied up a mass of skilled dockyard labour before they were finally written off.

I suppose I should have been wildly excited at the news from Malta, but I was completely exhausted after eighteen days of constant strain. I decided on an unusual experiment. I had wondered on occasion how the boat would manage if I got myself killed at sea. This does not mean I considered myself indispensable, but it did mean that Haddow, as first lieutenant, was lacking in command experience. I decided that my state of extreme fatigue would provide the opportunity of giving Haddow some of this experience.

I gathered the officers in the ward-room. 'I'm going to be Admiral for the rest of this trip. Haig will be skipper, Paul Thirsk Number One, and Tiger will navigate.'

I handed Haddow the recall signal and said 'Carry on, Captain. I'm going to be a very lazy Admiral and won't want to know anything. If we meet the enemy it will be up to you to take what action you consider necessary – even though we haven't any torpedoes left! – and inform me when convenient.'

All went smoothly, even when we ran into a convoy south-west of Marsala and sailed unpleasantly near an escorting destroyer. We dived swiftly to eighty feet, listened to their Asdics for a few minutes, and wished them damnation as they drew away. We entered QBB 255, and at noon on Tuesday, August 18th, we slid into Number One billet at Lazaretto, Haig Haddow still doing his stuff.

They gave us a royal welcome. The Malts lined the wharf, cheering, waving and shouting. They were happy. The convoy had got through, they had food to eat, and here was a submarine returning from a successful patrol. Our hearts went out to these valiant little islanders.

A galaxy of base talent was also waiting to greet us. There was 'Shrimp' giving a friendly wave, while next to him was Commander Sam MacGregor, the Engineer-Officer of the Base. Because of the manpower shortage, it was not an uncommon sight to find Sam aboard one of the submarines personally repairing a W/T set and solving the problems of a puzzled petty officer telegraphist. He described himself as the 'Garage Manager'. There was Giddings, Hubert Marsham, and the new Commander – 'Hutch' – Commander C. H. Hutchinson. At one time he was nicknamed 'The Gestapo' because, quite rightly, he put his foot down when a C.O. got above himself. His was an unenviable job, keeping order among a bunch of high-spirited submarine

116

skippers in their late and middle twenties. (Come to think of it, I'm surprised he tolerated my own idiosyncrasies, one of which was to stay in bed for forty-eight hours during each period in harbour.)

Among the others on the wharf were Joe Martin who had served with me as a midshipman and on the China Station, and who was at Malta in the capacity of spare C.O.

The outstanding personality was 'Shrimp' Simpson. He is one of the few men I have met of whom it is impossible to say an unkind word. Short, stocky, with gingerish hair and a dazzling smile, he had a wonderful sense of humour that was but seldom hidden beneath short bursts of irascible temper. He was a human dynamo with an endless source of energy who seemed to live without sleep in the Operations-room at Lascaris, his Lazaretto office, or walking around the island with a joke and a smile on his lips. He never in-convenienced anyone without good cause, although he was capable of tearing a miscreant to shreds in no time at all if the occasion warranted it. Above all, he was essentially approachable, a man without side. His C.O.s tried to live up to his example – although few could play hockey with this thirty-nine-year-old's gusto.

As soon as we secured, 'Shrimp' whisked me off for a verbal account of the patrol. As we talked, a flow of con-gratulatory signals poured in. They came from the C.-in-C., from the Vice-Admiral, Malta, from the Flag Officer (Sub-marines) London, and from Captain 'S' of the First flotilla. It was all very satisfying and head-swelling.

My interview with 'Shrimp' over, I handed the mainten-ance side to Sam MacGregor, informed the crew that we would not be going to sea for at least another fortnight, and had them fixed up with leave at one of the island's rest camps. These camps were the best bet for leave, for they provided the soundest value in food – still a very scarce item. 'Shrimp' had helped ease the problem by starting a piggery on Manoel Island, looked after by Giddings whose hawk eyes never missed a spoonful of gash. It was almost a capital offence in his eyes to throw a piece of orange peel into the water. As thorough with this job as with every task he undertook, he even persuaded 'Shrimp' to encourage first lieutenants of submarines to save gash on patrol and bring it back for his beloved porkers. By virtue of the smell of decaying gash in an air-rationed submarine, the scheme was not very successful, and the waste went overboard as usual. The grubby, muck-snouted pigs were our principal meat supply and seemed to thrive on anything thrown their way: bits of rock, old seaboots, paper, oily cotton waste – they gulped it down like animated incinerators.

There was practically no food or drink to buy, with the exception of naval rum. Thousands of gallons had been filched from the dockyard and become the staple drink of every bar on the island. Considering the risks involved looting the stuff, the price was reasonable. If this filching had been treated seriously, and 'steps taken', it would have antagonised every man, woman and child on the island, for a national failing among the Maltese is a marked predilection for the use of other people's property. There's nothing vicious about this: it is an essential part of the Maltese way of life. Having taken service with all the major Mediterranean navies since the Phoenicians, they have developed a tendency to share – albeit without permission – the possessions of their masters. However, British sailors are traditionally free and easy souls, and did not mind the pinching of their rum, especially since it provided them with the opportunity of drinking more than their daily tots at only moderate cost.

Some of the men preferred to stay at the base for their leave period, where they were excused all routines and came and went as they liked. Their favourite tipple was a mixture of rum and basic *ambite*, an explosive combination that produced monumental hangovers. Great believers in this jungle juice were the trio of Cryer, the Asdic operator, L.T.O. 'Bill' Scutt, and 'Pedro' Fenton, the gunlayer. Scutt was a tall, fair young man with a sharply-pointed nose who came from Hartley Wintney in Hampshire, while Fenton was short and dark and a native of Scotland. Cryer was a blond, burly Londoner.

On one occasion the three, dressed in overalls and carrying bottles of their beloved jungle juice, were apprehended by Hubert Marsham and run in. It appeared that when they were formally charged, the Master-at-Arms – the naval equivalent of a Regimental Sergeant-Major – suggested that although the jungle juice had to be confiscated it would be a pity to waste the stuff. Consequently there was a gay little party in a conveniently empty cell before the three malefactors were sent to me for punishment. I awarded them each thirty days' stoppage of rum, but I do not think it worried them unduly. They had ample stocks.

Surprisingly, perhaps, there was little fraternising between the lads and the local beauties, although one or two, after filling themselves with lunatic's broth in a boiled-oil shop did use their rations for a purpose regulations never intended. In the main, however, *l'amour* was kept on a vicarious level by the watching of highly professional clinches on the ten-year-old films shown at the local cinemas.

Two great 'characters' of Malta were 'Soft Joe' and the padre. The former was the nickname of Peter Harrison – now Commander Harrison, D.S.O., D.S.C. and bar – and it was largely of his own making.

When the sub-mariners got together in the ward-room it was only natural that we swopped tales of our exploits on the previous patrol, and Harrison's line almost invariably went like this:

'And there I was again – *having done nothing, mind you* – depth-charged all over the ocean . . . Poor old Soft Joe . . . Always the cane for him and none of the cream . . . Roll on Gibraltar . . . That's what I want: a single ticket to Gib.'

In point of fact he did damn well, and I shall never forget the look of amazement on his face when he described how he torpedoed, from very long range, a heavily escorted merchantman, without any comeback. He just couldn't understand it – nor could we when we worked out his plan of attack! It was true enough, none the less.

Padre Marsden was an Australian, and dished out really fierce sermons. One Sunday he delivered a scorcher about the evils of the bottle, then joined us for a couple of gins in the ward-room. He had several drinks and Joe Martin, remembering his threats of hell-fire and damnation, was puzzled.

'You know, Padre', he said, 'I don't quite get it. Half an hour ago you were shouting at us to lay off the stuff, yet I don't notice you drinking water.'

'Ah!' came the prompt reply. 'It was my duty to warn you of these evils.' He raised his glass. 'For myself I'll take a risk on it!'

Before church we had Sunday divisions, and on these occasions 'Shrimp' would address the men and tell them how things were going. One Sunday, however, we could see he was angry. It soon became apparent why. The lavatories had been freshly painted for the first time in years, and their pristine beauty had been defaced by one or two people whose desire for immortality seemed confined to having their initials engraved on a lavatory wall beneath a doubtful attempt at poetry. 'Shrimp' gave the assembled gathering a rip-roaring slating, then added:

'Only once in my life have I known anything funny to be written on a lavatory wall. If you can better it, well and good. If not, lay off the new paint. It went:

' "This bloody roundhouse is no good at all,
  The seat is too high and the hole is too small.'

'Underneath this was written, in a different hand:

' "To which I must add the obvious retort,
  Your arse is too large and your legs are too short." '

He brought the house down – and there were no more poetic efforts.

All in all, then, we enjoyed ourselves at Malta, the annoying presence of the air raids balanced by a regular flow of mail from home. Ting and June were still fine, and that was all I wanted to know. The future uncertain, I often cast my mind back over the happy times we spent together in the past, from our first meeting in October, 1940, aboard the *Britannic* returning from Suez to England round the Cape . . . Our lightning courtship . . . Our marriage in the Cathedral at Mombasa by special licence telegraphed from Nairobi . . . Our honeymoon in the half-empty ship . . . Our wonderful months together despite the gloom of the war . . . Her parting words to me: 'I won't think much of you if you don't come back. . . .'

But all good things come to an end, and our fun and games at Malta were brought to a halt with the arrival of Captain R. Wilson, D.S.O. – 'Tug' Wilson, the train wrecker. He had flown in via Alex, and we were to take him on his next escapade. Practising in a pond back home, using the motor of a windscreen-wiper, he had invented a new weapon – a mobile limpet. Actually it was a slow-speed miniature torpedo fitted with a special explosive of great power, which could be launched from a folboat and directed at its target. It avoided the danger of ordinary limpet-sticking which involved having to swim beneath the target to fix the explosive, but it suffered the disadvantage of having no time mechanism. This gave the operator a very short period in which to paddle away in his folboat. Our orders were to try out the gadget in the small artificial harbour of Cretone on the ball of Italy's foot.

On the same patrol we were to attempt a typical 'Shrimp' Simpson enterprise – torpedo a train!

There was, on the east coast of Sicily, a rail viaduct crossing the mouth of the River D'Argo. The plan was to fire a torpedo to set to run two feet deep – and oblique to the trestlework of the viaduct – just in front of an approaching train. The viaduct would be destroyed and a train would plunge into the river, all in one fell swoop.

Our orders laid down that we should investigate the train project, do Wilson's operation, bombard a railway siding thought to contain a number of trucks, then return to the viaduct. Quite a lark.

Before we sailed, 'Tiger' Fenton was taken from us. It was pointed out that he had been 'extra' to our complement, and there were plenty of demands for him from other, undermanned, submarines. By way of compensation we were given a fully qualified cook. This not only guaranteed a higher standard of meals, but meant that we'd have a trained baker to provide us with bread when stocks ran out.

By tea-time on August 31st we were ready for sea, and 'Shrimp' Simpson came to wave *au revoir*. With him was Joe Martin who yelled across the water: 'Lend me a fiver before you go. You won't need it.'

I thought it better not to have heard this, so I ordered 'Half astern together' and felt the familiar trembling of the engines beneath me.

Wilson was accompanied on OPERATION FOLBOAT by Bombadier Brittlebank, a huge, solid, powerful man of the type you want to have on your own side in a rough house. It was obvious that he would follow Wilson to hell and back. 'Tug' had none of Brittlebank's muscular bulk, being a slim and wiry fellow, radiating confidence. The two of them spent most of their time testing their weapons, of which they had a miniature armoury – three mobile limpets, Sten guns, grenades, knives and pistols.

For our part we carried only one item of gear apart from two folboats – a batch of dummy periscopes which we were to drop overboard in the southern approaches to Messina. Realistic-looking jobs, they would float around and create a jolly little panic when spotted.

*

On September 3rd we dived at 5 a.m. and closed the shore towards the town of Taormina in the shadow of Mount Etna. We found the River D'Argo and approached to within a mile-and-a-half of the beach. We saw the viaduct to be a gleaming modern affair with steel trestles resting on concrete piles. To my disgust, however, there was no water beneath the viaduct, only sand! Either the previous observers had seen it when the river was in spate, or they had been far out at sea and were deceived by the curvature of the earth. Since I could think of no way of making a torpedo cross land the project had to be abandoned. Flushed with the success of the previous patrol, we were not unduly upset by this minor set-back.

In a way 'Tug' Wilson and Brittlebank were disturbing passengers, for both were possessed of an all-consuming and morbid passion for their weapons of destruction. They crooned over them with their possessive love of unhappy mothers; oiling, testing, polishing, sharpening and adjusting. They seemed to regard sleeping and eating as no more than unfortunate necessities – cruel periods of parting from their adored ones. It was all very queer.

The plan for Wilson's operation was quite straightforward on paper, but was going to bristle with dangers in the execution.

R.A.F. photographs I had been given showed a 2,500-ton merchant vessel lying alongside the inner wall of the larger artificial harbour of Cretone. This was to be the target for Wilson's mobile limpet. We were to examine Cretone from periscope depth by day, measure the current, and then, when dark, launch Wilson and Brittlebank on their adventure. The two soldiers would be exposed to the greater hazards, of course, but it was not going to be too comfortable for the *Unbroken*. For, unlike 'neutral' Antibes, Cretone was an actively hostile port, and I did not relish the thought of loitering there. However, it had to be done, and that was that.

The activity around Cretone was confirmed as soon as we

crept towards the port early in the morning of September 5th. Through the periscope I could see that the town was dominated by a large chemical factory which belched heavy, bilious, yellow smoke over the harbour. Beyond the top of the mole it was possible to see, some two miles off, the masts of two ships. This was better than we'd hoped, for either would make an excellent target for Wilson and Brittlebank, and the fact that they were probably in the process of being loaded with chemicals would add considerably to the explosive destruction of a successful attack. I felt a pang of envy, for I'd have liked a crack at the factory myself. A few 3-inch bricks in the right spot might have blown the whole place to kingdom come.

During that day we kept watch on the town, observing the heavy rail and road traffic. Wilson scribbled cryptic notes on a writing-pad.

Finally he had everything worked out. He indicated the spot where we were to launch him, and made yet another check of the gear to be crammed into the folboat. It would be a heavy load, for apart from two men and three mobile limpets, the canvas craft would be weighed down with pistols, light automatic weapons, grenades, torches, and eight days' supply of food and water. It may sound crazy, but Wilson's plan, if he failed to keep his return rendezvous with the *Unbroken*, was to paddle back to Malta – all two hundred and forty miles!

'If driven to it', he told me, 'I'll take a coastwise course along Italy's sole, down the east coast of Sicily to Cape Passero, then hop the fifty miles across to Malta overnight.'

The day passed quietly until 7 p.m. Then, to my disgust, I saw one of the ships leaving harbour escorted by E-boats. I summoned Wilson to the control-room and beckoned him to the periscope.

'Our blasted targets look as though they're on the move. If they both come out your little caper will be off. I'll have a go instead with torpedoes.'

124

Wilson grunted. It was obvious he wanted the job of sinking the merchantmen all to himself.

I took the periscope from him. I watched carefully, and was able to announce: 'It's all right, the other one's staying in.'

'This game's too full of climax and anticlimax', murmured Archdale. 'I'm sure it's playing havoc with my health and strength.'

We laughed, and the tension eased. For the next two hours we stooged around, and at 9 p.m. surfaced in calm water seven miles from the harbour's breakwater.

A special Asdic and hydrophone watch was set for enemy patrol craft; extra look-outs were placed on the bridge. We gave the batteries the biggest charge the generators could produce, and shortly before eleven I ordered:

'Open fore hatch. Up folboat.'

Again that agony of waiting as we wallowed helpless and exposed. I peered into the still, moonless night while the folboat party hauled the clumsy canvas to the casing. All was quiet and dark, save for an occasional dull red glow from a factory chimney.

'Fore hatch shut and clipped, sir.'

'Lash the boat and clear the casing.'

This done, we trimmed down to reduce silhouette.

'Group down. Full ahead together.'

As we approached the breakwater, Wilson joined me on the bridge. 'I've decided to negotiate the passage through the main boom, not the breakwater', he told me. 'They may have blocked the breakwater. If you can get to a mile off the end of the breakwater, I should say the job will take us no more than an hour and twenty minutes.'

I muttered my assent. We both knew the snags, and it was pointless to repeat them. Once his limpets struck home the alarm would be given. It would take him twenty minutes to get back to us, and all that while he would be hunted with every device at the enemy's disposal, including searchlights and E-boats. The Italians had often been attacked by impudent folboatmen, and their thoughts would immediately fly to a submarine lurking beyond the breakwater. I knew that Wilson and Brittlebank would do all they could to make their attack succeed, even though success diminished their chances of survival, and I felt an uncomfortable lump in my throat.

By now we could smell the acrid smoke from the factory chimneys.

'Slow together.'

'Fifteen cables to go, sir.' Thirsk's voice sounded strange as it came up the voice-pipe.

'All right. Give me ten, seven, five, then each cable.'

'Aye, aye, sir.'

'Tell the first lieutenant to get the casing party up to prepare to launch the boat.'

The night had cleared a little. Stars could be seen high in the heavens, and a few dim lights stared from the darkness. It was still very quiet. The casing party moved quickly and silently in gym. shoes. Brittlebank went below to collect the gear and provisions.

'Five cables.'

The end of the breakwater loomed up dead ahead, bearing due west.

'Stop both.'

As we came to a standstill the folboat was launched. After I wished Brittlebank *au revoir* he climbed down to the casing.

I turned to Wilson. 'We're close enough now. You've a mile to go due west for the end of the breakwater. When you've left I'm going to turn round and take a position three thousand yards from the end of the breakwater. This will give us a better chance in the event of being hemmed in by patrol craft. If you fail to make this rendezvous because we've been chased away, steer due east to the dawn rendezvous five miles off the breakwater. If we do not meet there, continue due east and we'll be on that line.'

'That's fine.'

'Well, so long and good luck.'

A quick handshake and he was over the bridge and on to the casing. Silently the two men manned their boat and disappeared into the night.

The *Unbroken* gathered sternway.

7

AFTER we turned and took up our amended position, Archdale, Osborne, the two lookouts and myself commenced our vigil. Apart from the gentle lapping of the sea against our side, the Mediterranean night was quiet and still. Thinking of cool English beer and the rustle of summer dresses, I sighed as I peered into the darkness. Our eyes were glued to our glasses, while our ears strained to catch any unusual noise, although there was no guarantee we would hear the limpets strike home. Wilson had argued that the breakwater, plus the special construction of the limpets would muffle the explosion.

The minutes ticked by. Wilson and Brittlebank had left at eleven-forty. We expected them back at one.

To our annoyance the chemical factory started to lay down a heavy screen of acrid smoke. I cursed, for if it became too thick we would not be able to see the flash of Wilson's torch when he signalled his return.

Midnight. Restless, one of the look-outs started to hum softly the opening bars of 'Rule Britannia', broke into the 'Toreador's Song' from *Carmen*, then lapsed into unhappy silence. I lowered my glasses to rest my aching eyes and wished I could light a cigarette.

The night remained unhappily quiet. A thousand doubts and fears nagged at my brain. Had their overladen folboat been sunk? Were they prisoners of the Italians? Perhaps

E-boats were preparing for a sudden dash from the harbour, with searchlight crews ready to bathe the sea in light . . . I rubbed a hand across my eyes. *I'll be cracking up if I go on thinking like this.*

Twelve-thirty. Still no sign or sound of Wilson and Brittlebank. To keep to their schedule, the explosion must come now, for it would take them half an hour of fast paddling to cross the mile and a half of sea that separated us. . . .

I whispered down the voice-pipe: 'Control-room time?'

'Quarter to one, sir.'

Perhaps his infernal machines have gone off without us knowing. But surely there would have been a flash, even though the break-water muffled the sound? . . . Curse this bloody smoke! I turned to Archdale. 'Maybe they had some trouble with the boom.'

'It's possible, sir. He was going to take things very carefully because the place was so lively today.'

'We've stacks of time before the moon comes up,' I said, 'but I wish to God I knew what was happening across there. It must be – '

'Flash from harbour, sir! Looked like an explosion!'

I swung my glasses. As I did so there was a second eruption of red fire. But no noise. It appeared that Wilson had been right when he said the sound of the explosion would be muffled.

'Thank Heaven for that.' But even as I spoke a searchlight beamed across the water. The instinctive desire was to duck as it swung towards us, but it was switched off as suddenly as it had come on.

'What now, sir?' asked Archdale.

'I wish I knew', I replied. 'We've just got to hang on and hope.'

The next thirty minutes passed in an agony of silent terror. There was no torch signal from Wilson, no dull shape loomed from the darkness. He could not have missed us if he had kept to instructions and steered due east. I leaned over the bridge and whispered into the night: 'For God's

9   129

sake hurry,' but the only reply was the monotonous lapping of the sea, as patient and remorseless as time. . . .

'What's that?'

A vague, indefinite noise to starboard. A moment later it cleared to become the throb of a high-speed engine.

'Fast H.E. to starboard.'

The game's up! But I said nothing, determined to hang on until the last possible second. I was conscious of Archdale's eyes on the back of my neck, but I refused to turn. I held hard to the side of the bridge, bit my lip and stared towards the shore.

'Vessel on starboard quarter,' yelled the look-out. 'Approaching fast.'

It was no good. We had to think of ourselves. I crossed to the voice-pipe. 'Klaxon! Klaxon!' The helmsman swore and pressed twice the button of the klaxon. As its harsh, ear-piercing stridence roared through the submarine, the two look-outs swung themselves through the conning-tower hatch and slithered down the ladder into the control-room. As Osborne followed the vents opened, and the bridge shuddered with the whip of the propellers. I shut the voice-pipe cock and took a last look at my enemy. An E-boat, doing good speed. Within a minute she would pass directly over us.

As Archdale's head disappeared down the hatch I ordered: 'Sixty feet. Shut off for depth-charging.'

'Sixty feet. Shut off for depth-charging', he repeated. I hurried after him and prayed that in the darkness some clot aboard the E-boat had mucked up the depth-charge firing mechanism.

At forty-five feet Haddow ordered: 'Blow "Q".'

The noise of the air as it screamed to the quick-diving tank almost drowned Osborne's: 'Lower lid shut and clipped, sir.'

'Sixty feet, sir,' reported the cox'n.

'Boat shut off for depth-charging,' reported Manuel. I nodded.

I mopped my forehead, swallowed, and waited for 'the heat'. But nothing happened. Maybe I had been right, and some numbskull had forgotten to remove the safety-pins of the depth-charges.

I beckoned to Telegraphist Morris. 'Let me know when we've been down five minutes.'

'Aye, aye, sir.'

The five minutes dragged past.

'Port twenty. Steer oh-eight-five. Group down. Slow together.'

Then, from Cryer: 'I can hear pinging, sir.'

Hell and bloody damnation! I had not expected modern anti-submarine craft with Asdics at a piddling little port like Cretone. If they chased me all over the ocean, no rendez-vous would be kept with Wilson and Brittlebank – assuming they'd got away. I took a pair of earphones. Cryer was right. There was no mistaking the sound of Asdic impulses. We were in for a hunt.

'Silent routine.'

Cryer moved his automatic Asdic control-knob slowly around the compass. There were two enemy craft. Both had Asdics. I crossed to Paul Thirsk and examined the chart over his shoulder. The water was not very deep, restricting our movements, for we did not want to run aground. There was nothing for it but to sweat and endure.

The enemy started hunting us in earnest, but we remained slow and silent and it took them twenty minutes to estab-lish contact. When they did, both ships were to port, and I had just the sea room for a bold alteration of course to starboard. This put the enemy astern and ourselves heading back towards Cretone. They did not guess what we were up to.

By 3 a.m. things were quieter, but still disturbing. For the enemy was combing the sea to eastwards – where we wanted to be to meet Wilson. I decided to describe a wide circle which would bring me to the saboteur's escape route at dawn. By then the anti-submarine vessels should have cleared off.

At 7.30 a.m. we were at periscope depth and ten miles from Cretone. The day was bright and visibility good. We used both periscopes – one to keep watch on sea and sky, the other searching for the folboat. But the sea remained despairingly empty – until 8.20 when a couple of anti-submarine schooners sailed from the harbour.

We kept to our course for another ten minutes, until we were seven-and-a-half miles due east of the breakwater. If Wilson and Brittlebank had escaped along the planned route they would certainly have got that far by now.

The schooners began dropping depth charges, and it seemed they were going to comb the entire area in this manner. Reluctantly I decided to call it a day. There was no more I could do for our gallant friends. I ordered a withdrawal towards the south-east.

In the ward-room, while the events were still fresh in my mind I wrote it all down. My hand was tired and my heart heavy by the time I reached the words: 'The loss of this brave officer and his companion is very much regretted, and it is hoped the submarine did all possible for their recovery.' Then came the saddest duty a Captain knows: writing a letter to the next of kin. I begged Mrs Wilson to believe me when I said that I was certain her husband would get through, either by escaping, or as a prisoner-of-war.

As it turned out, my optimism was justified. A long time afterwards I discovered that the saboteurs had penetrated the boom after their limpets had exploded – although not, alas, against the ship – but the subsequent chase had been too hot for them. When they realised they would not be able to contact the *Unbroken* they put into operation their plan for paddling back to Malta, but were captured en route. This, however, was not to be revealed until many months later, and we sailed south-east from Cretone mourning the loss of two outstandingly brave gentlemen.

Next evening we crept towards the shore where the River

Amendolea meets the sea near Cape Spartivento, and where we were to bombard the railway sidings. Subdued after the loss of Wilson and Brittlebank, my spirits were in no way improved at the sight of the sidings completely bare of trains and trucks. It appeared that this patrol was to be a long succession of disappointments. To add to my ill temper a torpedo-boat appeared some miles off, apparently bound for Reggio. But as we moved away from her we spied a handsome-looking railway bridge, and I decided to have a go at that even though the torpedo-boat might turn around and investigate the gunfire.

After the gunlayer and trainer had been given a peep at the target through the periscope we surfaced, and without wasting time opened fire.

In six minutes we pumped thirty-seven rounds at the bridge, a third of them hits. Others exploded on the railway lines, while a few overshot the target and made useful holes in the motor road beyond. It is difficult to destroy a bridge with a 3-inch gun, but it is possible to weaken it. This, I felt, we had done, and if we put the line out of action for twenty-four hours it was as good as sinking a 5,000-ton merchant ship.

As the bombardment compromised our position in no uncertain manner, I thought the time ripe to dispose of our dummy periscopes. They would not be seen that night, but enemy forces searching for us next day would waste a mountain of depth charges attacking them. We dropped them about twelve miles apart. The product of Sam MacGregor's ingenuity, they resembled exactly the British bifocal jobs.

The bombardment of the bridge did much to vent our pent-up feelings, and having acquired the taste for short, sharp gunnery, I set sail eastwards towards the Gulf of Squillace where another railway line was to be found.

We reached the gulf next afternoon, and admired its beauty through the big periscope. We also found a quiet stretch of line between two tunnels. The track was set low down but ran for most of its length over culverts and via-ducts. Our plan was simple: to knock a train from one of these viaducts. There was an unfortunate drawback – all afternoon we saw only one train pass. We could but hope, so we surfaced at eight o'clock, closed to within half a mile of the shore and waited.

High in the hills above the railway ran a winding, rolling road, and to our delight and surprise we saw many cars pass along it with their headlights full on. The thought struck me that if the worst came to the worst we could put in some gunnery practice on a Fiat, but I dismissed it as somewhat barbaric.

Two-and-a-half hours passed without even the distant whistle of a train and I was biting my nails and cursing the irregular services of the Italian railways. It was pitch dark, and I did not fancy loitering much longer. It was quite possible that some smart Alec in a near-by defence position had sighted us through night-glasses and was madly phon-ing the whole Italian Navy. To be caught by patrols and flattened against the shore might provide an experience I would be unable to retail to Soft Joe over a glass of ward-room gin. I decided, therefore, to bombard the empty line and tear up some tracks.

It was going to be a difficult shoot, for the gunlayer could not see what he was aiming at. To help balance this, we had taken aboard a stock of flashless star shells to go with our flashless high explosive, which meant we would not blind ourselves with muzzle flash. It meant, too, that the enemy would be unable to see from where we were firing.

The gun's crew closed up and I stood with Archdale on the bridge. 'Can you identify anything at all?' I asked.

'Absolutely nothing, sir, except the skyline.'

That was of no help for the skyline topped the wooded hills high above our heads.

'Well, we'll have to open up with star shells, then seize on the best target they reveal.'

'Aye, aye, sir.'

'Control-room! Broadcast that we're going to open fire at the track in the absence of a train.' To Archdale: 'All right, open fire.'

The gun roared and a star shell screamed into the air. A second followed. The echo and reverberations were tremendous. It seemed the entire mountain range was cracking open.

The shells burst into dazzling golden light and parachuted slowly to earth. But the scene they illuminated was vastly different from the one we'd expected.

'I can't see any railway line, sir,' shouted Archdale.

Neither could I. 'Can anybody see it?' I asked.

Out of the corner of my eye I saw the port look-out switch over to see the fun. 'Not you! Back to your sector!'

'The line's not in sight', said Archdale. 'Of that I'm certain. It must have gone into a tunnel.'

That was it. We had drifted a little northwards and were opposite the side of a tunnel. Archdale pointed. 'How about that road culvert high on the right, there?' he asked excitedly. 'There's a car crossing it now.'

I gave my assent and we managed to fire two rounds at it before the star shells burned themselves out. Much to our joy the car came to a halt and the driver, in his panic, forgot to switch off his headlamps, giving us a useful point over which to aim our star shells. For all this the shoot was more spectacular than accurate for the culvert was high up and its range uncertain. It was impossible to make spotting corrections as we were unable to see the shells burst, and those that missed fell like thunder-claps into the ravine. In all, eight star and fourteen high-explosive shells were fired. We may or may not have scored a couple of hits on the culvert, but the star shells certainly started a very promising forest fire. After five minutes I decided to discontinue our Crystal Palace display, and withdrew. As the burning countryside receded in the distance, we felt as gleeful as naughty schoolboys on Guy Fawkes night.

Next day, soon after we received orders to return to

Malta, Joe Sizer the coxswain came to see me. Compared to the rest of us, he was positively elderly, for he was not far off of his fortieth birthday. Bald and short, he was the most impassive of men, possessed of a reassuring north-country calm. On this occasion, however, his sharp-featured face was wrinkled and disturbed.

'Sorry to bother you, sir, but a great chunk of the frozen meat's been stolen from the fridge. I reckon someone doesn't approve of good meat being returned to the base. . . . What I was wondering, sir, was whether you'd authorise an issue of tinned meat to replace the stolen stuff.'

My reply was immediate. 'Certainly not. The stolen meat has probably been eaten by more than one man. The ship's company will go without meat until the amount's made up.'

It was, I knew, an unpopular decision, but it produced a surprise result – the meat mysteriously reappeared and was eaten for supper.

The incident upset me, for it showed a surprising lack of any sense of responsibility on the part of the wrongdoers. Food was pitifully scarce at Malta, and every ounce had to be measured in the blood and suffering of the Royal and Merchant Navies. This may sound pompous now, but the grimness of the situation was very real at the time. I remember Chief E.R.A. Manuel telling me bread was so short in his mess at the base, the president ordered a ration of one slice per man per meal. A thin slice, too, and he illustrated his point by pinning a sample to the notice-board.

In the main, however, stealing was rare aboard the *Unbroken*. A favourite prize was the ward-room silver. Piece by piece it disappeared into the engine-room where the stokers and E.R.A.s whiled away the hours filing it down into natty submarine brooches. The point came when we were almost reduced to eating with our fingers, and Joe Sizer had to make good the loss by bribing a Malt in the dockyard with a pound note and a bag of sugar to supply us with silverware salvaged from the sunken *Pandora*.

Our stay at Malta was marked by the departure of Soft Joe Harrison who finally got his one-way ticket to Gib. Bob Tanner did the thing in style, handing a genuine railway ticket stamped with the words: 'Malta Express Railways.' Soft Joe examined it doubtfully. 'Hmmm', he muttered, 'third class and no seats guaranteed . . . Poor old Soft Joe . . . Always the cane and none of the cream. . . .' On this occasion his moan was to be justified, for his boat was nearly sunk by our own forces outside Gib. Poor Old Soft Joe!

It was when Bob Tanner gave me a ticket stamped 'Misurata' that I had my first indication we were to go on another patrol. With a name like that I was glad it was a 'return'.

The patrol was to be off the African coast in search of shipping plying between Tripoli and Benghazi, and we set to sea at 3 p.m. on September 25th after eleven days in harbour. We were escorted down the swept channel by the minesweeper *Rye* in the company of the *Una* and the unchristened P.34. The latter was taking Soft Joe to Gib., while Pat Norman in the *Una* was to patrol south Italy. We parted company near Filfla Island, the *Rye* returning to Malta, the three submarines diving and fanning out to west, south and east.

We surfaced after sunset and battled towards Misurata in a south-easterly gale. The sea was angry, and a high swell brought blankets of water crashing over the bridge. Soaked and miserable, I left Archdale to suffer in solitude and repaired below for my tot of rum with its complementary halibut-oil pills for night vision.

I peeled off my wet clothes, slithering across the wardroom as the boat rolled and pitched. I cursed, and yelled for Butterworth.

His lanky form staggered into the ward-room. I struggled into a pair of old flannels and white submarine jersey. 'See if you can get these wet things dried behind the engines – and try, just for once, to bring them back without being either smothered in grease or burned to cinders.'

'Yes, sir.' He took them with the resigned dispassion of a Jeeves in reduced circumstances. I noticed he had a napkin across his arm, waiter fashion.

'What's for supper?'

'Corned beef, sir.' As an afterthought: *'Fricassée.'*

I raised my eyebrows. 'All right. We'll have this gastronomic masterpiece in twenty minutes.'

He lurched out.

Haig Haddow pulled a gin bottle from a locker. 'No rum, sir. The tot tonight will have to be gin.'

'And why is that?'

Haddow smiled guiltily. 'Sorry, sir, all gone.'

'I suppose there was a party at Malta to which I wasn't invited.'

'Oh, no, sir. Not a party. Just a few drinks.'

'Like hell.' I stretched my legs and lighted a cigarette. The first 'bine of the day was invariably evil-tasting. The foul air of the submarine clung to the tobacco and poisoned your lungs. This could be negated in part by the insertion of menthol crystals in the end you puffed – but only in part.

I felt unusually relaxed for a first night at sea. This was invariably the time for doubts and qualms, a moment to worry about the unknown future, a period in which to yearn for the comparative safety of Malta.

'What do you think we'll find down in the desert, sir?' asked Haddow. 'Not much traffic down that way.'

'No, but what there is is important.'

'The trouble there is lack of water,' piped up Thirsk. 'Too shallow.'

'Anyway,' said Haddow with feeling. 'I'd rather be in the shallow water off the desert than in the deep sands on it.'

'By the way,' I said, 'you can start a little eager speculation among the crew by letting it be known that certain of us have been recommended for decorations.'

'Really?' said Haddow. 'Any idea who's going to be lucky?'

'None at all. Although "Shrimp" did indicate that my

own modest brilliance has not been overlooked.'

At that moment half a sea crashed into the control-room and Butterworth skidded into the ward-room, a cup of soup grasped in each hand.

'Twenty minutes was what I said, Butterworth.'

'I know, sir. I'm sorry, sir. I thought I'd better bring it while there was some left.'

'I suppose', said Haddow acidly, 'every rating has already had two helpings.'

'Oh, no, sir', came the innocent reply. 'Not two. It didn't run to more than one-and-a-kick each. Everybody's very hungry. Nothing to eat in harbour. This sea puts an edge on appetites.' Pointedly, he added: '*Some* people's appetites.' He marched out, ever the suffering martyr.

As he left, Ordinary Seaman 'Trampy' Mullet, the control-room messenger entered. Automatically I rose to my feet and wondered what had happened.

'Any of you gents got a match?' he asked. 'All ours is wet.'

We looked at him, then at one another, dumbfounded. Haddow was the first to recover. 'Here you are, Mullet,' he said, handing over a box. 'Next time, please ask someone else.'

Mullet took the box, nodded and disappeared.

'This place is becoming a mad house,' said Thirsk.

Mullet's main duty was assisting Cryer. Both he and A.B. John Jones kept a listening watch on the Asdic and acted as control-room messengers when such a watch was unnecessary. A Hostilities Only rating, Mullet had been working on a farm only six weeks before joining the *Unbroken* at Barrow, and when given his first spell at the wheel his comment was: 'I'm a cowhand, not a navigator.' Transferred to the Asdic, he was very useful, for he had extremely acute hearing. As Manuel put it, 'he could hear the green grass grow.'

We ate the corned beef, euphemistically labelled *fricassée*, and washed it down with coffee. Then Haddow inquired: 'Have you heard about our rat, sir?'

'Are you slandering a member of the crew?'

'No, sir. This is a real rat. It's been seen dodging around the boat. The boys have hung up a cigarette-tin in the control-room and every time the rat is seen the spotter puts a penny in it. They say it's to buy the beast a motorbike when we get back to England.'

'I suppose that's one of Master Cryer's bright ideas.'

'I'm not certain,' replied Haddow, 'but I've discovered one thing about Cryer. He's got a weakness.'

'God, don't tell me he keeps pressed flowers between the sheets of a signal-pad.'

'No, sir. It's art.'

'Eh?'

'Yes, sir. Art.' Haddow fished in his pocket and drew out a folded sheet of paper. 'He presented me with this.'

I took it and saw a drawing that was certainly spirited if not skilled. It represented a scene of wild panic in the control-room with myself the central figure. I looked across at Haddow. He had developed a sudden intense interest in the tips of his finger-nails. I grunted, and reached for the Night Order Book.

At the top of the page was a small circle. In it was written the figure 108 – our hundred-and-eighth night at sea since leaving Barrow.

To my annoyance we were called on October 2nd before we'd had a chance of a crack at the enemy. But our patrol was enlivened by an ugly little incident in the Gulf of Sirte.

I had closed to within four miles of the port in search of shipping, but the cupboard was bare. As I turned the boat around to leg it seawards, the stern started to drop. Such behaviour was not unusual when turning, but on this occasion the damn thing went on dropping!

Something was caught round the port screw. Something very strong. A wire, in fact. There are only three sorts of wire that catch a submarine's propeller – net wires, buoy wires and mine wires. There were no nets or buoys around.

'Diving stations!' I called. 'Midships. Steady as you go!'

A glance at the control-room gauges showed we had been dragged stern-first from periscope depth to forty feet. In a moment we would be bumping the bottom. 'Group up! Half ahead together!'

I was in a sweat. Our only chance was to speed the propellers and hope to God they severed the wire. If that didn't work we'd be held in a vice-like grip on the sea-bed – if the screws didn't get smashed up by a tougher-than-usual wire. For an absurd moment I remembered an item of cold comfort I had once been given: 'Death on the sea-bed is quiet and gentle. The air grows worse and worse until you finally feel drowsy and fall asleep. . . .'

With a jolt that almost shook my teeth from my head, the *Unbroken* broke free. The boat shuddered and planed upwards. . . . I felt sick in my stomach.

CHAPTER

8

I KNOW it is considered bad taste to refer to medals in any terms save those of self-depreciation – *Frankly, old boy, I don't know why they gave it to me* – but the honest fact remains that once a chap knows he's due for a 'gong' he's impatient to get it. He wants to pin it up before he bites the dust. Vanity? Arrogance? Conceit? Perhaps. But no worse than mock modesty and hypocritical humility. I remember discussing all this with Lynch Maydon, skipper of the *Umbra*, on our return to Malta, and we consoled ourselves with the thought that the Powers that Be had more important matters to occupy their minds.

After leaving Lynch, I sipped a gin in the Lazaretto ward-room and ran through the 'U'-class Captains between his boat and mine – P.35 and P.42. Seven boats had slid from the Vickers launching stage – there being no P.40 – and Lynch and myself were the only two left. Of the others, four had been killed and one relieved. God had been good to me, and that, I reflected, was more than compensation for the late arrival of a couple of ounces of ribboned enamel.

Tension mounted as the Eighth Army stiffened its sinews for El Alamein, and Intelligence reported that Rommel was frantically scraping every pint of petrol and ton of armour he could from the Axis High Command. The duties of the submarines at Malta were plain; to prevent convoys from crossing to North Africa and to stop enemy sea traffic between Tripoli and Benghazi. Rommel saved some six hundred miles' worth of petrol for every lorry shipped in this manner, and the economy was worth more to him than blood.

The rebuilt 10th flotilla was now quite strong, comprising the *Umbra, Una, Unbroken, Unison, United, Unrivalled, Utmost, Unruffled* and *Unbending*. In addition we were aided by several submarines, such as the *Safari*, which rightly belonged to the 8th flotilla.

United and *Unbroken* were ordered down the African coast east of Tripoli to have a crack at coastal traffic. Co-operating with us were R.A.F. Wellingtons and Swordfish of the Fleet Air Arm.

At about tea-time on October 11th we parted company with the minesweeper *Speedy* at the outer end of the swept channel and dived on a southerly course. The days were drawing in, and we were able to surface before seven. The sky over the northern horizon was its familiar red, and I looked across Paul Thirsk's shoulder as he wrote in his notebook: 'Air raid visible at thirty or forty miles. Feeling well out of it except for £40 left in my upstairs drawer.' These wealthy bachelors!

Two days later his entry read: 'Entered patrol area north of Khoms. Made landfall and closed land. Expecting fairly quiet time.' He may have been a Vasco da Gama when it came to plotting stars, but he should have left forecasting their astrological significance to Lyndoe, for his 'quiet time' turned out to be the closest shoulder-rubbing with Death we had known.

The following day we sighted a 4,000-ton ship escorted by torpedo-boats and shagbats,* well to seaward. For an hour we chased them, but they drew away. Later we heard thirty-seven distant explosions in groups of three to ten. Depth charges. It seemed as though *United* was getting the heat.

*Aircraft.

We surfaced as soon as we dared in order to break wire-less silence and inform Malta of the merchantman's course. Later we saw distant flares as our aircraft combed the sea in search of her. Then came a signal from 'Shrimp' saying she had been damaged by an aerial torpedo and that *United* and ourselves were to go in and finish her off.

We altered course towards the position of the crippled ship as reported by our aircraft. I hoped the Fleet Air Arm boys were accurate, although it would be understandable if they were not, for they were operating in the dark, two hundred and fifty miles from base, with nothing on which to fix their positions save unidentifiable desert and sea.

We dived early and at six-five I was called to the control-room to see a *Partenope*-class torpedo-boat coming out of the sunrise straight towards us. My instinctive desire was to dive deeper, out of her way. Then, remembering there was a shortage of likely targets in the area, I decided to attack her. As we started the attack I was nagged by a little voice in my brain that warned me I was behaving foolishly. Destroyers and torpedo-boats were not targets for a submarine. They were the cats to our mouse when it came to assuming combat roles. In any case, a British submarine was worth ten of them in terms of war potential. If I missed and the come-back was fatal I would let the side down with a bang. . . . However, as this particular boat was not zigzag-ging she provided too tempting a target to miss – even though she had her Asdic switched on and might pick us up. On the other hand, of course, she could pick us up whether we attacked or not.

My worries were resolved for me, for when still two miles off the torpedo-boat turned about and returned from whence she came.

At 10 a.m. Malta came through to inform us the merchant vessel was stopped and floundering ninety miles to eastward. As I'd feared, the position given the previous night had been inaccurate. We swung round to eastwards and hurried on, only to suffer another spasm of enraged helplessness. For in the afternoon, four small vessels, including a tug and a decrepit gunboat, waddled past. They were clearly going to the assistance of the damaged supply ship off Ras Khara. They were too small for torpedo targets, but as I prepared to surface to demolish the tug by gunfire, an aircraft wheeled into view. I stomped about the ward-room cursing heartily, until a further signal from Malta directed us to a new position off Khoms. It was estimated that dawn would bring the tug, merchantman in tow, sailing past us.

But dawn brought neither tug nor merchantman. Signal followed signal, and we spent the entire day chasing backwards and forwards across the ocean, tempers deteriorating with each new alteration of course. Frustrated and angry, we swore and fumed, until 'Shrimp' came through with positive information that our quarry was beached off the Khoms anchorage. We were to torpedo her there, using just one kipper.

In the ward-room I examined the charts in company with Thirsk and Haddow.

'The place should be free of mines,' I said, 'although that's pure guesswork on my part. The main trouble is that we'll have to operate in water less than fifteen fathoms deep. Not only will our line of escape be restricted in depth, but in direction as well.' I ran my finger along the chart. 'Look. After firing there's only one course we can take – turn about and aim for the sea along the path we used coming in. The enemy won't need to be very good with his Asdic to pick us up. They'll know we must be hopping it along a nice straight line at ninety degrees to the coast. It's the only place we could be.'

'The trouble with this coast', said Thirsk, repeating his theme song, 'is that the water's too bloody shallow.'

'How about currents?' asked Haddow.

A good point. In a normal attack, the target, torpedoes and submarine are equally affected by tidal streams and currents. Thus the problem cancels itself out. But when a ship is aground and therefore fixed to the shore, the current

10

can make all the difference.

'As no one here has any local knowledge of Khoms,' I said, 'that problem is in the lap of the gods.' I thought a moment. 'The general set is south-east, isn't it?'

'Yes, sir,' replied Thirsk.

'That doesn't mean a thing as there are usually counter-currents in these coastal indentations and bays. I'm inclined to allow nothing. Then the error will be only half what it would be if we allowed, say, a knot in the wrong direction.'

A tortuous piece of reasoning, but it was the best I could do.

Our spirits were bucked at having a positive destination after buzzing around like drunken bluebottles. But the sight of Khoms through the big periscope had a sobering influence. For one thing the sky was alive with shagbats, indicating that the enemy put a high value on the crippled merchantman's cargo. Tanks, probably, or motor vehicles. Then a torpedo boat hove in sight and started to patrol between ourselves and our target. Her Asdic transmissions were reported by Cryer with disturbing frequency.

The merchantman was beached a few cables off Khoms' main lighthouse. She had a list of ten degrees to port, and her bows pointed east. A schooner lay alongside, while a tug and a second schooner stood by some yards off. It appeared the enemy were investigating the situation to decide whether to attempt to refloat the crippled vessel or remove her cargo and leave her there.

The shoaling waters made a close approach impossible, and the inaccurate charting of the surrounding coast made it extremely difficult to fix our position with the precision the situation demanded. As we crept in I glanced round the control-room, and could see that no one liked the set-up. Nothing was said, there were no signs of panic – simply an almost imperceptible stiffness of bodies and tightness of lips. I thanked my lucky stars I had not yet encountered the moment of panic beloved by film producers when a man rushes to the conning-tower, screaming: 'Let me out! Let me out!'

Joe Sizer and 'Rattler' Morgan, his second, were as steady as granite as they rotated the planes and kept us at the ordered twenty-seven feet. There was no cheeky grin on Cryer's face as he struggled to maintain contact with the torpedo-boat. His forehead was furrowed and he was plainly worried. I could guess the cause: the water noises along the sea-bed, only a few feet beneath us. Haddow's face was solemn as he leaned over the backs of the planesmen, grasping the conning-tower ladder for support. Occasionally he twisted round to transmit a trimming order on the telegraphs to the pump operators huddled in the bilges.

Archdale was bent over the chart table, feverishly active. Somewhere behind me, Manuel hovered, while Telegraphist Morris was squeezed against the steering-wheel clutching the control-room log with one hand, a pencil at the end of a piece of string in the other. As orders were given he recorded them in the log with the furtive haste of a bookie's runner.

Nervously, ginger-haired Osborne rubbed a piece of brasswork in no need of a polish.

In the ward-room passage Butterworth, his face white and serious, stood ready to check vents and pass messages for'ard.

Aft, beyond the dead and silent engine-room, Scutt leaned with deceptive nonchalance against the wooden guard rails between the main motor switchboards, his eyes glued to the telegraphs.

I saw all this in one hurried moment, and transferred my attention back to the periscope. I shared the common uneasiness, but hoped I did not show it.

We nosed slowly into the shallow water. The trim was perfect: depth twenty-seven feet and not an inch either way. I turned to Haddow. 'What's the sounding?'

'Fourteen fathoms, sir.' That was the overall depth of the water – twenty feet of it above the casing, fifty-odd feet of it below the keel.

'Cryer! Watch carefully for the torpedo running. It may easily hit the bottom. . . . Stand by Number Three tube . . . Starboard ten . . . Steer two hundred.'

We swung sluggishly, and I became too engrossed in the job on hand to experience further doubts or qualms. The torpedo-boat was still patrolling without suspicion. We were within range of her Asdic now, but as we were nearly bows-on to her, we made a small target for its beam.

'Number Three tube ready, sir.'

'Very good.'

'Course, sir, two hundred.'

I took careful aim at the merchantman's funnel.

The steering was steady. I was dead on. A sitting shot.

'Range?'

'Five thousand, sir.'

'Fire Three! Down periscope!'

'Torpedo running, sir.'

At that second, as I clipped up the periscope handles, I saw the torpedo-boat steaming away to eastwards, one aircraft over the target, another coming towards, a third circling Khoms. I was thankful the muddy water would conceal the torpedo track.

We waited, creeping further into the unfriendly shallows. . . .

'Up after periscope. What is the running time?'

'Running time, three minutes twenty seconds.'

The seconds seemed minutes, the minutes hours. I wiped my damp forehead with the towel round my neck.

'Four minutes, sir.'

Not a sound. I'll try just one more. 'Stand by Number Four tube. Down after, up foremost, periscope.'

Crossing from one to the other I looked at the depth gauges. They were as steady as if they had been welded to the dials. 'Nice work, Number One. Keep it up.'

'Number Four tube ready.'

I gazed at the scene ahead. The periscope's magnification was such that my field was almost restricted to the target, the lighthouse behind, the schooner alongside and the tug. No sign of alarm. Once again I fixed my sights on the wretched ship's funnel.

'Fire Four.'

The discharge raised our bows.

'Down periscope.'

The bubbles on the inclinometer's gauges leapt for'ard. We were coming up.

'Speed her up if you have to,' I told Haddow. 'We can't afford to break surface here.'

A moment's anxious pause, then: 'It's all right, sir. We've got her.' The bubbles stopped their forward movement and crept back to a central position.

From Cryer: 'I can't hear that one.'

Blast and hell! The bitch has hit the bottom. She's stuck in the mud there. . . . That's why the other didn't explode. . . . Oh damnation! . . . I was told to fire one kipper into this wreck. I've fired two and they've both missed. What now? Shall I come back tonight? If I do I can creep in to within a thousand yards for a certain hit. On the other hand a hit from a thousand yards would bring a torpedo-boat on to us at a spot where we wouldn't be able to dive. Not worth the risk. In any case I probably won't be able to get into such a favourable position again. . . . All right, one more, and one more only.

'Stand by Number One tube.'

I crossed to the after periscope and waved it upwards with my hand. 'Sounding?'

'Twelve fathoms, sir.'

God's teeth, we'll be aground in a moment! 'Hurry up the tube.'

'Number One tube ready, sir.'

'Clamp me on zero.'

Manuel gave the periscope a slight twist. 'On now, sir.'

'Fire One.'

The boat bounced.

'Down periscope. Half ahead together. . . . Hard a-port.'

'Torpedo running, sir.'

'Up after periscope.'

The range had been four thousand yards. Running time: two minutes, forty seconds. We sank slowly as we turned.

'Forty feet, sir.'

'All right . . . Slow together. Bring her up to twenty-eight. I want to see.'

Mullet screwed round on his stool at the wheel. 'What course, sir?'

I looked at the chart. 'Where's the pencil?'

Osborne rummaged in the bilges under the chart table.

'Hasn't anyone got a bloody pencil?' I roared.

Morris, sensing my rising anger, quickly jerked his from the control-room log and passed it over.

I fiddled with the chart and parallel rulers. As I'd anticipated, there was only one course to steer: back along the road that brought us in. 'Bring her round to oh-two-oh.'

'Two minutes thirty . . . Forty . . . Fifty . . . Three minutes, sir.'

I swore aloud. 'Haig, tell the boys we've missed and we're getting out of here.'

Twenty-eight feet. Through the after periscope I could see a flap around the merchantman. The schooner had cast off and the tug was flying some sort of signal. As we had not scored a hit, they must have seen the torpedo track pass close. I took a look at the torpedo-boat. She was still going away.

We slipped off without trouble.

That evening in the ward-room we held an inquest. 'Maybe I should have taken your advice, Haig,' I said. 'The current must have foxed us.'

'Half a knot of current or half a degree's error in the torpedo course would make all the difference,' said Archdale.

'Spilt milk,' I muttered. 'Perhaps we should have fired a fourth. . . . How are the boys taking it for'ard?'

'I think they're too relieved to be out of the shallow waters of Khoms to care much about us missing,' said Haddow.

'I don't blame 'em.'

P.O. Willey came in. 'Excuse me, sir. Immediate from S.10.' With his customary impassiveness he handed me the pink signal slip.

It told us to proceed to a position off Lampedusa. There had been considerable activity around the north coast of Sicily and an important convoy was expected to move southwards across to Africa that night. All available submarines were to close in on it.

I handed the missive to Archdale. 'Plot it and give Thirsk the new course and speed.' He nodded and went out.

A few minutes later I heard him call up the voice-pipe to the bridge: 'Officer of the Watch, please.'

'Thirsk here.'

'From the Captain. Alter course to three-one-seven. Zigzag "B". Three-three-oh revs.'

I turned to Haddow. 'Spread the buzz, Haig. It'll cheer the chaps up a bit.'

That night there was a constant hustle between the wireless office and the ward-room as signals from Malta detailed the convoy's strength and course. There was one large tanker, brimming over with petrol, and four supply ships swollen with tanks and motor vehicles. Escorting them were seven of Italy's most modern destroyers, and more aircraft than our observers could count. Their course appeared to be taking them from Sicily across to Pantellaria, then past Lampedusa and Lampion to Tripoli.

Further signals gave the position of our own forces. While *Unbroken* and *United* were closing in from the African coast, *Safari* had sailed hurriedly from Malta to join the attack. *Utmost*, commanded by 'Basher' Combe, and *Unbending*, skippered by Edward Stanley, both returning to Malta after successful patrols, had been diverted to give us a hand.

'Shrimp's' final signal pointed out that the destruction of the convoy could make 'all the difference' to the war in North Africa.

We dived at dawn and by ten o'clock were in position between Lampion and Lampedusa. After a hurried meal I sat in the ward-room impatient for some sign of the convoy. But all was quiet until 2 p.m. when *Utmost*, taking a suicidal risk, surfaced to signal that the convoy was just beyond our horizon. Although we did not know it at the time, *Unbending* had sunk one of the escorting destroyers at eleven that morning.

As soon as the signal came through from *Utmost*, I hurried to the control-room, took over the periscope and had the boat shut-off for depth-charging. Five minutes later I saw a smudge of smoke on the western horizon. My heart leapt. Quickly I ordered a change of course towards the enemy.

Twenty-five minutes later we started the attack, our target the oil tanker. Near her were a supply ship of some 7,000 tons, and two smaller vessels, while four of the destroyers circled round throwing up huge white bow-waves. I could see but three of the escorting aircraft. Hindering our attack was the elaborate, irregular zigzag course of the convoy. Twice as the time of firing approached they turned away from us. Then, as I feared they would continue their second turn-away, they swung back.

'Down periscope. What track* am I on?'

'A hundred-and-ten degrees, sir.'

Tricky. 'Stand by all tubes. Up after periscope.'

In the small attack periscope the target, four miles away, was invisible, but I could see one of the aircraft flying uncomfortably close.

The convoy was slightly off our starboard bow now with one destroyer sweeping round between ourselves and the target. Another destroyer raced along astern of the first, while a third suddenly swung round and approached us bows-on. If she kept to this course she would almost certainly scrape our stern.

The sea was too choppy for us to keep depth at any speed less than four knots, while waves splashed the periscope

*Track angle: the angle at which a torpedo approaches the target.

obscuring my vision. There was only one way of continuing the attack – stick about five feet of the big periscope out of the water and hope to God the aircraft did not spot it.

'Down after periscope, up foremost periscope. . . . Director angle?'

'D.A. green eleven,' said Archdale.

'Down for'ard periscope.'

The enemy's speed was only eight knots which would necessitate a long interval between each torpedo. To reduce this I decided to fire as the submarine swung to starboard. It meant that each torpedo would have to be fired by eye – I could not fire the first by eye, then go deep and fire the rest of the salvo on a calculated time interval – but the result would be more accurate.

Time was growing short. To add to my worries the nearest destroyer was no more than a thousand yards off. She would be on top of me in sixty seconds, and a good look-out should already be able to see my 'big stick' when it shot out of the water. None the less, up it had to go.

'Up for'ard periscope. Starboard ten.'

I saw nothing but water splashing the periscope glass. I cursed roundly. 'What's the depth now, Number One?'

'Twenty-six feet, sir.'

'Bring her up to twenty-four. I can't see a bloody thing.'

'Coming up . . . Twenty-four feet.'

'Half ahead together.' Time was vital. The enemy were right on top of us. But I soon forgot these things as my sights came on the tanker. There was only one motto for a successful attack: Fire first and worry later.

The periscope was fixed between the tanker's mast and funnel.

'Stand by. . . . Fire One!'

The *Unbroken* bounced as the torpedo shot into the water.

'Fire Two! . . . Fire Three!'

My sights swung on to one of the supply ships. 'Fire Four!' I swallowed. My salvo was fired. I swung the periscope, very aware that I was viewing the situation from the top of a long pole sticking high above the surface of the sea.

Jesus! To my horror I found myself looking straight into the cockpit of a seaplane in a steep bank. 'Down periscope! Group up! Seventy feet!' As I clipped home the periscope handles I saw a vague shape drop from the aircraft. I shot out my hand and pressed the klaxon for an emergency increase in depth.

A bomb? I waited, stiffened. . . . No, not a bomb: a marker – and we were now only three hundred yards from the leading destroyer.

'Hard a-port', I called. 'Steer one-five-one. Full ahead together.'

The air screamed from 'Q' tank.

'All torpedoes running, sir.'

Down, down, down. There was nothing left but prayers and hope.

In the torpedo compartment Petty Officer Lee chalked on the tally board the four torpedoes fired – making our total twenty-five – and waited expectantly for the sound of an explosion. But he did not stand idle. He checked that one of the doors to the tube space was properly clipped, saw all was ready for closing the other door in a hurry, and moved his torpedo-firing party to their depth-charge posts in the torpedo compartment where the last kipper of the patrol lay in its rack. Here they would work the fore 'planes if 'local control' was ordered. Above them were the two hatches which might well be the first places to crack open if a depth charge fell too close – the fore hatch through which the torpedoes were brought aboard, and the for'ard escape hatch. On my orders this was always kept firmly clipped from the outside. No one would ever escape through it. We would sink or surface together.

Abaft and below the torpedo party, the for'ard pump worker squatted in his damp, stinking steel dungeon in the bilges, mechanically stopping and starting the ballast pump at the dictates of the electric telegraphs.

Butterworth crouched between the crew space and ward-room, ready to pass forward messages from the control-room.

In the W/T office, between the control-room and the engine-room, John Willey tried to take his mind from the grimness of the situation by concentrating on a new set of codes and ciphers shortly to come into force. Beside him, signal-pad and stop-watch ready, Johnny Crutch waited to record the bangs.

E.R.A. Leech was in charge in the engine-room where he kept a watchful eye on the rating working the after ballast pump. There was little else for Leech to do save share the general discomfort and fear. The engines were well shut off. He draped himself across an engine casing and hoped for the best.

Further aft, Scutt and his 'winger' stood fiercely con-centrating on a mass of ammeters, voltmeters, repeaters and thermometers, as well as telegraphs. The motors whirled beneath their feet.

Right after in the tail, unseen and alone, squatted a stoker. Doubled up in the narrow stern space, his teeth rattled with the vibration of the propellers. He watched the steering and after 'plane motors, with an occasional unhappy glance at the quivering hull above his head.

Scutt and his assistant were the lucky ones. They were too busy to fear for the sound of depth charges.

'What's the depth round here, Archdale?'

'Difficult to say, sir.' He turned towards me. 'It's badly charted. Something between twenty-three and thirty-four fathoms.'

'What's the bottom?'

'That's a bit vague, too. Might be sand or shingle. Possibly even coral.'

There was no time to reflect on the shortcomings of the hydrographers for Cryer roared across the control-room: 'Enemy in contact. Starboard beam. . . . Another destroyer red one-five-oh. Seems to be in contact, too.'

I licked my lips and gnawed at a thumb-nail. *The bastards are certainly close enough.* The supposed supersonic transmissions of their Asdics were clearly audible in the boat.

From Cryer: 'Revs. increasing. Destroyer on port quarter coming in to attack.'

One destroyer was holding us in contact, directing the other to the attack.

From the volume of the noise of our screws the enemy knew we were doing top speed and would make suitable allowances for his depth charges. We must dodge.

'Group down. Slow together. Silent routine.'

A distant, tinny explosion made us all jump.

'A torpedo hit,' reported Cryer. For a moment I relaxed and smiled. Then came the sound of a second kipper striking home. Five minutes had passed since the moment of firing.

Whatever happens to us, we've left our mark.

From Cryer: 'They're slowing down, sir. One destroyer on each quarter. Both in contact.'

If anyone wants to make peace with his Maker, now's the time to do it.

The first depth charge was too close for comfort, and the next three were even closer. The destroyer on the starboard quarter had crossed our stern to join the other on the port side, dropping her eggs in our wake as she did so.

'H.E. all round,' said Cryer, and as he spoke we heard the familiar noise of an express train tearing from a tunnel as a third destroyer rushed over us to join the attack.

There was a half-minute of silent apprehension, then a great *clang* on the casing. A depth charge had scored a direct hit but, by a miracle, had failed to explode. A moment later it went off below the ward-room, together with three others in the salvo.

An inferno of ear-splitting, bone rattling chaos was let loose: a lunatic confusion of crashing glass and cursing men as the submarine was turned into a monstrous cocktailshaker. In the middle of it all, darkness, as every electric-light bulb in the boat was smashed in its socket. A shower of cork from the deckhead rained down. The shock would have thrown me from my feet had I not grabbed at the control-room ladder. The luminous depth-gauge needles jumped from their frames and hung drunkenly useless. Gauges throughout the boat were shattered. I started to lose balance, and was temporarily paralysed with fear as I realised the bows were dipping. *We're sinking. This time we've had it. My God, Ting, I've let you down. . . .*

CHAPTER

9

TORCHES were switched on. I pulled myself together and looked across at the barometer glass. It did not look broken. I tapped it. It moved. A slight increase of pressure; no more. The hole could not be a large one. We had a chance.

Manuel stumbled through the gloom. 'It's all right, sir. These boats can take it.'

The spell was broken. 'Thanks, Chief. Check up quickly all round, will you?'

He nodded and went aft. The indicator of 'Q' tank flickered. Somehow it had flooded. A moment later an explanation came when the engine-room reported: 'After pump hull valve shut.'

'*What?* Who the hell *opened* it?'

'They say it jumped open two turns. It's all right now, sir.'

The shock of the explosion had opened hull valves – had worked the wormwheel against the worm, supposedly a mechanical impossibility – and water had poured in to lower the bows.

Haddow brushed against me. 'Shall I blow "Q" now, sir?' He was as calm as if we'd experienced no more than a jaunt on a roller-coaster.

'No,' I replied. 'Mustn't blow. They'll hear it. Put the after pump on the midship tank, and pump like hell from for'ard with the for'ard pump. It'll need some pumping.

We must have shipped a good few extra tons of water. . . .
We've got to pump like fury to stop our bloody bows from
going down any more. I wonder how far we've dived? Try
and get a depth from for'ard. . . . Half ahead together.'

From Sizer: 'After 'planes out of action, sir. I can't get
any response from them.'

There was a second rattling convulsion as fresh depth
charges crashed down.

'From aft, sir. Defect on port main motor. Will you stop
it, please?'

'Stop port, full ahead starboard. After 'planes in local
control.'

'Depth gauges for'ard and aft all smashed, sir,' reported
Haddow.

'Leech!' He came running from the engine-room. 'Open
up a pressure gauge on the engine circulating system and
get me a depth.'

Someone stuck a bulb into a socket and we had some light.
At least the fuses hadn't been smashed. But we still had
enough trouble on our hands.

From the engine-room: 'Depth, sir, one hundred and
sixty feet.' Were we scraping the bottom? No one could tell.

The light in the electric bulb began to dim. 'From the
motor-room, sir, large drop in voltage.'

The batteries! We had forgotten them in the stress of the
moment. Before I could pull my wits together, Sizer
reported: 'After 'planes are now in local control but they
still aren't responding.'

'Tell Leech to go aft and try to find out the trouble.'

'Report from the motor-room, sir. Port main motor field
regulator gearing smashed. Trying to clear it.'

Butterworth poked his head into the control-room.
'Batteries gassing, sir.'

'Thirsk, take a hand and examine the main battery
bilges.'

I sniffed. An acrid smell of gas. Slowly it became stronger
as the choking fumes seeped eerily through the boat.

At that moment another pattern of depth charges crashed into the sea. They were a little way off. Another pattern exploded – even further away.

'I think they've lost contact,' said Cryer.

So we'll choke to death instead of drowning.

The voltage continued to drop. The life in our batteries was ebbing fast.

Jones moved over from the Asdics. In silence he handed me a slip of paper. I screwed up my eyes to read it in the fading light.

JONES, John. Able Seaman. D/JX 254129.
Request to go back to General Service.

I grinned and passed it round the control-room. If we'd had our chips, there was no harm dying with a smile.

By this time, despite the uselessness of the after hydroplanes, we were managing to stagger along. Their absence, however, caused us to curve up and down like a switchback at between a hundred-and-twenty and a hundred-and-seventy feet.

The gas was tickling my nose and scratching my throat. Two more charges exploded to port. 'Only two,' I murmured. 'Perhaps they're running out.'

Manuel arrived from aft. 'The starboard shaft is revolving quite sweetly,' he reported, 'and there are no leaks aft. They'll not be long with the port motor, but you won't be able to vary its speed much.'

Archdale came to report there were no leaks for'ard, either.

Cryer could still hear Asdic transmissions, but it appeared the tornado was over. We described a large circle to starboard then drew away to the north-west.

A single ashcan went off in the distance. I glanced at the control-room clock. It had stopped at 3.26 p.m. I looked at my own watch: 3.40. It seemed impossible that only fourteen minutes had elapsed since we stood on the threshold of eternity.

The poisonous smoke from the batteries continued to seep through the boat, lying heavily just above the level of the deck. I reckoned that if it did not increase its speed of discharge we would surface before it had a chance to choke us. On the strength of this assumption I allowed myself to relax a little.

We were still alive, and the boat had suffered no serious injury. It was, in its minor way, a miracle, and I thanked God for his mercy. We had been as near to death as was possible without actually kicking the bucket, and I remembered with a wry smile Paul Thirsk's expectations of 'a fairly quiet time.' And as I thought of Paul I felt very proud of all the boys aboard the *Unbroken*. Their behaviour had been magnificent. There could be no praise high enough.

At 4.20 p.m. I was given a verbal report of the conditions of the batteries. There was a considerable amount of acid in the two sumps, showing that cells in both batteries were broken. There were – praise heaven! – no signs of salt water to produce chlorine gas. Number Two battery, however, was on fire, and had started giving off heavy smoke. The poisonous fumes, the smoke, and the heat of the fire tainted the thick, heavy air with choking foulness. Again worried, I ordered that distilled water should be hosed over the burning battery to keep the temperature down. The men doing the job were issued with respirators, and I wondered how long it would be before we all wore them.

An hour later we bumped and jolted to periscope depth. Nothing in sight. The light was fading. We surfaced, and I climbed through the conning-tower in the cool calm of the Mediterranean evening as though I were struggling back to sane reality after a bout of nightmare delirium.

As I stood gulping the clear, fresh air, the T.G.M. reported that our remaining torpedo appeared to be in good order. After the pounding I doubted whether its delicate mechanism was still working, but as it was impossible to strip the brute right down I ordered him to have it loaded into a tube.

No one at Malta knew yet of our pasting, and they brightly sent a signal ordering us to patrol off Kuriat the following day. I read it and shrugged. *Why not? We can just manage to dive. There's a torpedo of sorts left, and we've got a gun and plenty of ammo.*

Signals told me the convoy had reformed after 'dispersing in confusion', and aircraft from Malta reported that one damaged vessel was being escorted back to Lampedusa by one of the destroyers. She was the second of my torpedo targets. (Next day she was found by Ben Bryant in the *Safari*. Dodging her escort he sent her to the bottom with a well-placed kipper, and as she sank it was seen that her upper deck was crammed with motor transport.) The Malta aircraft could find only five destroyers. There having been seven when the convoy set out, and allowing for the one sunk by the *Unbending*, it was thought a fair probability that one of my torpedoes sank the other as she swept around the convoy. But we never really knew, and claimed only to have damaged the merchantman.

I ordered a course westward towards Kuriat, and went below for a fuller examination of our wounds. I found we weren't out of trouble by a long chalk.

As I made my way below I hoped we would be able to disconnect Number Two battery and complete the patrol on Number One, but when I reached the motor-room I discovered Number One also on fire. This did not mean that flames were licking our feet. The battery fires were electrical, a red hot mass of metal cell plates and boiling acid setting alight the vulcanised wood of the cell containers. Lack of air in the batteries prevented the smouldering mass from bursting into active flames, but the temperatures of the batteries were rising fast and the poisonous, blinding smoke poured out with increasing density. It was clear we could not dive again without terrible risk.

'Tell the officer of the watch to alter course to one-eight-oh. We're going home.'

I left the electricians to deal with the batteries as best they could and made for the ward-room to draft a signal to Whitehall for onward transmission to Malta. Outlining our troubles, I said that the damage was greater than was at first supposed, and that it was unlikely we would be able to dive at dawn. Because of this I requested fighter cover from the first light of day. I added that we could not expect to make Valetta until the middle of the afternoon.

Soon after the signal was sent all hopes of diving next day were completely shattered: the fire in Number Two battery became so fierce we would certainly suffocate if we did not keep to the surface. In any case, gas masks or no gas masks, it was no use diving if there would be no electricity to turn the motors.

With the ventilation running flat out we managed to grab a cup of soup and a bite of tinned meat for supper. We ate as best we could, sharing the few plates that had not been smashed in the uproar. The decks were scorching beneath our feet, and Scutt spent his time spraying the boat with distilled water. When this gave out he switched to fresh water, of which we still had a good supply.

Examination showed there was not even the smallest of leaks in the hull. I had fully expected that hundreds of rivets would have been sprung, even forced out. But no. Once again I thanked the men of Barrow.

None of us slept that night, despite our extreme weariness, for no one wanted to take a chance on being gassed in bed. Intead, the men off watch crowded into the control-room and found some little relief from the lung-poisoning smoke in the draught that blew down the conning-tower.

After I had eaten I climbed to my deck-chair on the bridge. The night was moonlit with a gentle northerly breeze. The danger of E-boats forced us to zigzag while the moon was up, and we kept a look-out for a U-boat which had been reported in the area. To confuse matters, we expected *Safari* to cross our path while legging it after the remnants of the convoy.

Nor could we forget the trouble below. The battery ventilation outlet was at the after end of the boat's superstructure, and the light following wind wafted the sulphurous yellowy-green smoke over the bridge.

Shortly after midnight we received a signal from 'Shrimp' saying we would be met at dawn by a motor launch and that fighter protection would be provided.

Six hours to go.

The look-outs were doubled, and we limped on.

Then, as I sat huddled in my chair, thinking over the events of the past day and wishing I could close my eyes and sleep, a voice called out: 'Object bearing red seven-oh.'

I jumped up and grabbed my glasses. As I did so the 'object' sailed into the moonlight and I recognised the silhouette of the *Safari*. She recognised us, too, and turned away. With a sigh of relief I slumped back into my chair.

Never was a friendly face so welcome as that of Lieutenant John Peel when he drew alongside in M.L. 121. A moment after his arrival an aircraft swept across the sky from the grey dawn over distant Malta.

By nine o'clock everyone below had to wear gas masks. Number Two battery was disconnected, for it was now a bubbling cauldron of molten metal, gas and steam. For the sake of those whose jobs kept them below, the fore hatch was opened, and the remainder of the crew came up top and squatted on the casing. By the time we reached Lazaretto at two in the afternoon, smoke was billowing from the conning-tower as though from a factory chimney.

As the *Unbroken* was nudged into dry dock the seams amidships opened and Number Two battery was flooded with salt water. Chlorine gas filled the boat. Once again we had escaped disaster by the skin of our teeth.

It used to be said among experienced skippers that a submarine could withstand an attack in which a third of her battery cells were broken, but none had been known to withstand the loss of more than half. That was understandable when you consider the amount of force needed to destroy battery cells. Each of the *Unbroken*'s weighed a quarter of a ton, and we carried 224 of them. By this reckoning half weighed twenty-eight tons. If there was enough force to destroy twenty-eight tons' weight of cells, there was enough force to sink the boat.

I had this in mind as I watched the workmen remove the shattered cells from our batteries. The 112 cells of Number Two battery were an unrecognisable mass of molten junk, and it took the men three days to shovel it out. From Number One battery a dozen cells were removed. A total of 124 cells – thirty-one tons' weight.

Yet we had survived.

Back at Lazaretto I collected my mail. In it was a telegram saying my younger brother, a fighter pilot, had been killed on active service the previous afternoon.

The previous afternoon. . . .

It took them four weeks to knock the *Unbroken* back into shape. Every day I visited the dry dock and gazed sadly at her plates, buckled by the force of the depth charges. As Scutt remarked: 'They should change her name from *Unbroken* to *Badly Bent*.' Paul Thirsk had the task of keeping a watchful eye on the repair work, and when we finally prepared for sea again I decided to give him and some of the ratings a rest from the next patrol. For myself I thought it best to carry on. The boys, I felt, trusted me, and a new skipper takes some getting used to. In any case, since they had to go to sea next patrol, why shouldn't I?

On October 23rd General Montgomery launched the mighty battle of El Alamein, and in the weeks that followed our submarines were busy tearing holes in the enemy's convoys to North Africa. Only the crippled *Unbroken* was left at Malta, and I felt miserably out of it. Then, on November 8th, the invasion of North Africa, and the Germans poured supplies into Tunisia with every ship at their disposal. Fighting was in full swing by the time we set sail on November 15th, fully repaired and almost as good as new.

This patrol lasted twenty-one days, and from the point of view of strain was the worst we had endured. We were only depth-charged once, but were chased backwards and forwards across the ocean with maddening constancy, and without an iota of success.

We all felt pretty shaky when we sailed. The memories of that last patrol were unpleasantly fresh in our minds, and we knew the enemy had intensified his anti-submarine efforts. To add to the normal hazards coastal radar stations had been established to pick up submarines on the surface at night. The enemy did his job well, for we were unable to do anything on that patrol without being made to dive, made to dive deeper, hunted by Asdics or bombed by aircraft.

On the first night out, as we approached QBB 255, I was lying on my settee, queasy and unable to sleep, when I suddenly felt wet and jumped up. The officer in the top bunk jumped up, deeply apologetic. He had been sick – and it wasn't seasickness.

'It's all right, chum,' I said. 'You're not the only one feeling that way.'

In all, we sighted two thousand enemy aircraft on that patrol. Time and time again, when at periscope depth, I would feel the bows go down. A visit to the control-room invariably brought from the officer of the watch: 'Going deep, sir. The sky is absolutely lousy with shagbats.'

On one occasion I was in the heads when a loud *whooomp-pha!* caused me to rush to the control-room with my trousers still down.

Haddow was going deep. With a wide grin he said: 'Sorry, sir, it was that Junkers – the one you said would be all right. He changed his mind, banked around and pranged us. Or tried to.' Later we were hunted for three hours.

It was like that for three weeks. Even at night we could

only surface for short spells because of the presence of E-boats and aircraft. It was not difficult for the enemy to hound us like this, for our patrol position was only a few miles from his naval ports. One night, to give everybody a rest and to get some juice into the batteries, I withdrew from the coast and reported the situation to 'Shrimp'. I suggested the uncanny persistence of the enemy was due to one or more of three things: shore radar, radar-equipped aircraft, or that our own ciphers were compromised. 'The fury of the enemy,' replied 'Shrimp', 'is because you are in his way! Try patrolling position. . . .' As the new position was only a few miles from the old one, this was cold comfort, but I was just able to see the joke.

Towards the end of the patrol, we intercepted one of those signals we dreaded: '*Utmost*, report position.' She did not report her position. She could not. She had been sunk by an E-boat off Marittimo. Another fine bunch of sub-mariners had been lost, and I mourned for a personal friend in 'Basher' Coombe, her captain.

Joe Martin was at sea in the *Una* while Pat Norman took a rest. He followed *Utmost* into the trap. A suspicious type, Joe never under-estimated the enemy. One night, while sitting in the ward-room, he had 'a sort of feeling' and hurried to the bridge. He saw a white streak in the water. 'Hard a starboard!' he roared. 'Get down!' *Una* dived on the turn – and the torpedo just missed them.

This put an end to the well-known route back to Malta past Cape Granitola. When we were due to return we were told to take a new course. It started by the Skerki Bank and struck, in deep water, through the Sicilian Channel to Pantellaria, skirted that island and ended up towards Linosa. Unable to take sights, with soundings of no help, and with our log broken down, we had to make a blind rush through the new lane. Our luck held, and on December 5th we were escorted back into harbour.

With feeling I wrote at the end of my report: 'This has been *Unbroken*'s most arduous and disappointing patrol.'

The only person to profit from it was Lieutenant Craw-ford, Paul Thirsk's relief, who added a little grist to the mill of his experience.

Paul Thirsk certainly had the laugh on the rest of us, for he'd spent the patrol period amusing himself at Operational Headquarters, Lascaris. I saw later that he commented in his note-book: 'Rejoined *Unbroken* after a pleasant month on the beach. Sorry to leave Lascaris, the lovelies and nightly drink in Charlie's at Sliema.' Apparently he had been neg-lecting that golfing jacket of his.

Back at Malta I discovered we had developed a 'singing' propeller. This was a serious business, for although the propeller was still quite efficient, it hummed a tune which would delight enemy Asdic and hydrophone operators. We were docked for a quick change, but none of the spares at Base fitted properly. The old one had to go back on. It was asking for trouble, but what else could we do? In any case, having learned that we had been sunk three times by the German radio, we were now feeling rather cocky.

We were stuck with our singing propeller until the end of the commission. It was the port one, and when hunted by enemy Asdics it became necessary to stop the port motor and proceed on the starboard. A nuisance, but it saved our skins.

Christmas was to be spent at sea, and we sailed from Malta on December 20th under a dark, threatening sky. Before we left we were asked if we would rather take our festive luxuries with us, or wait and have a slap-up feed on our return. We decided on the latter, knowing Joe Sizer had scrounged a plum pudding and a suckling pig, while a few bottles of beer had been wheedled from a reluctant Naafi. All being well, therefore, we would have two lots of 'big eats' for Christmas. There was great speculation as to how Sizer got the pig, but we thought it best not to probe the question too deeply.

We set course past Pantellaria, and after skirting Marit-timo proceeded across the Tyrrhenian Sea towards the Bay of

Naples. On the night of December 22nd, soon after surfacing, enemy ships were reported. We dived and I commenced a periscope attack on the nearest one. In the moonlight it seemed a fair-sized supply ship. As we closed, however, I realised I had run into yet another anti-submarine sweep of destroyers. I tossed up in my mind whether to take a risk and attempt to sink one of these pests when a signal was rushed to me in the control-room. Received the moment before we dived, it had just been decoded. It said: 'All submarines clear out of an area within fifty miles of Marittimo.' Things were getting hot. I consoled myself with the thought that supply ships, not destroyers, were top priority on our list.

We described a wide circle, and when we surfaced on the night of December 23rd after dodging an E-boat patrol, we were back again on a course towards the Bay of Naples.

On Christmas Eve our feeling of peace and goodwill was destroyed by the hordes of enemy aircraft that continually swept over the horizon to plague our lives. When this air activity continued into Christmas Day I felt I was justified in seeking a little peace twelve fathoms down. Asdic conditions were good, and if a target did pass close enough to warrant an attack we could soon come up to periscope depth and wham home a kipper.

Until evening there was little to distinguish Christmas Day from any other on patrol. Then the roast pork and plum duff were passed round, washed down with a bottle of warm Malta beer. Joe Sizer was less meticulous than usual when measuring the rum ration, and we were all mellow and nostalgic by nightfall. I sat in the ward-room feeling sentimental and a little sad, yarning over memories of other Christmases – traditional occasions of snow and holly, punchbowls and log fires . . . Christmas beneath a tropical sun when 'out foreign' . . . The first Christmas of the war patrolling in the submarine *Regulus* in search of U-boats off Vladivostock . . . Christmas at Barrow with Ting . . . I thought of her and the child I had not seen, and wondered what sort of a Christmas they were having amid the bleak damp gloom of a Suffolk winter.

Then, from the control-room, a carol softly sung. In spirit, at least, 'Trampy' Mullet was back with his folks on the farm. *Silent night . . . Holy night . . .* As I listened, it gave me a sensation of unreality, for there is a certain incongruity about such things when you are in a stinking, foul-aired submarine, the thick, oil-heavy atmosphere smarting your eyes, the sound of angry water slapping the hull beside you, engines clattering noisily, your clothes unchanged since leaving harbour, and eight sleek and shiny torpedoes ready to tear the living guts from your fellow humans. *Silent Night . . . Holy Night . . . All is calm . . . All is bright . . .* For the dozenth time I re-read the last letter I had received from Ting before leaving Malta. I stretched out on my bunk and shut my eyes. The singing had stopped. For a moment I felt sick and unhappy.

10

Boxing Day saw us moving across the Gulf of Naples between Capri and the island of Ischia. The forenoon was cold and clouded, and shortly before midday smoke was reported on the horizon. We closed towards it, and I saw an enemy force consisting of two merchantmen escorted by an armed merchant cruiser. The larger merchant vessel was of some 6,000 tons, and I thought I'd make the boys a Christmas present of it.

The convoy was sailing out of the gulf with the obvious intention of creeping round Ischia's Imperatore Point as close inshore as possible. It took us an hour to reach a firing position, and I dispatched four kippers from a range of thirteen hundred yards. The A.M.C. interfered with my aim, for she was weaving ahead of her charges on a wide, sweeping zigzag. I fired just as she changed from a zig to a zag and was only three hundred yards away from us. We went deep and heard the satisfactory sound of a steel-tearing explosion. Then, the cheering over, we waited with the tension of dreadful memory for the *krrrump* of depth charges, but the cruiser failed to pick us up. Nine minutes after firing she dropped a pattern of four, but they were well away from us.

Thirty minutes later we nosed up to periscope depth. Our victim was bows down in the water, fifty feet of her sharp end missing. She was going down. There was no need to waste another kipper. The second merchantman was wallowing back to Naples, escorted by the A.M.C.

I reasoned the area would soon be a beehive of anti-submarine aircraft and ships, so we set course to the south – and the electric railway line in the Gulf of Policastro.

We found an excellent target not far from Acquafredda: a red brick viaduct, a hundred yards in length, running across a ravine between two tunnels. The structure was set a quarter of a mile back from the coast, but as the water inshore was good and deep, I reckoned on a gun range of no more than a thousand yards. At one end of the viaduct stood a power house and signal station. This would make a fine secondary target, the primary one being the arched pillars of the viaduct, each sixty feet high.

It was encouraging to note that if our shoot was successful the position of the viaduct and power house between the tunnels would make them extremely difficult to repair.

The days were short and sunset was at 4.45. In order not to be trapped by enemy patrol vessels sweeping round the gulf I intended to remain submerged until a train came out of the tunnel, then pop up and knock it from the viaduct. With the aid of a large-scale chart we went over the details in the ward-room.

'You can take charge of this shoot,' I told Thirsk. 'It's all experience. We'll work on the assumption that the train will bowl out of the tunnel at twenty miles an hour. All right?' He nodded. 'Good. The viaduct is a hundred yards long. A hundred yards at twenty miles an hour? . . . Come on. Who was last from school?'

'Ten seconds,' said Archdale.

'Brilliant! If the train is two hundred yards in length, for how long will we have some of it in the target area?'

'Thirty seconds.'

'Right. That gives us a chance. From the order "Surface" to the first round, twenty seconds. That leaves ten seconds in which to get a hit. The margin is small, but we'll have a try. We'll close up at four o'clock, leaving two hours for a train to put in an appearance before it's too dark to see.'

At first, after closing up, we were restless with excitement. Then, as time passed, boredom crept in, to be replaced in turn by restlessness of a different kind: the cramped impatience of being too long on one's toes, waiting for an order that did not come. My eyes ached as I peered into the periscope, for it was impossible to relax. Thirty seconds was all we would have if a train appeared, and each was vital.

The light faded. With a sigh I straightened my stiff back and turned to Thirsk. 'Too late for trains. We'll surface and knock out the power station. That will stop the alarm being given. Then concentrate on the centre arch of the viaduct.' To Haddow: 'Don't forget a double set of look-outs. We don't want to be trapped by patrols crossing the gulf.'

The gun's crew, huddled in the conning-tower, came down to stretch their legs. Fenton and his trainer had a last look at the target through the periscope.

'We'll surface, stop the motors, and drift slowly towards shore. This will give you the best chance as there will be no control complications caused by our own movements.' I turned to the control-room in general. 'If trapped by patrols during the shoot we may have to dive astern. It can't be helped.' A complicated manoeuvre, but I thought we could make it. Indeed, we would have to make it.

'All right, everybody?' Heads nodded and thumbs went up. 'Right. Close up again.'

The gun's crew returned to the conning-tower.

'Bearing green three-oh. A power house. Range one thousand. Deflection zero.'

The instructions were repeated back.

'Surface! Open fire when ready!'

The air screamed through the pipes to Numbers One and Six main ballast tanks.

The first round was fired as I was still climbing the conning-tower. It took but six more to reduce the power house to a shambles, crackling electric flashes inside the power house adding to and confirming the success of the shoot. The overhead wires came down and performed a death dance on the rails.

'Switch target!'

The range now was nine hundred yards and we were practically stopped, bows towards the shore five hundred yards away. I glanced quickly over my shoulder. The look-outs, with commendable self-control, were busy sweeping the sea and sky behind us. The rate of fire was good: seven rounds a minute, each carefully aimed. Shells slammed into the parapet of the viaduct and the main structure below. Great clouds of red brick dust were formed with each explosion, and they hung almost motionless in the air. We were using, for economy, ordinary 'flashing' ammunition, and I wondered whether anyone in the valley beyond the viaduct had spotted the red spurts of fire. To a person ashore the scene must have been macabre. The lovely small bay flanked by steep green hills and dominated by the viaduct. The white-flecked blue of the sea deepened by the clouded sky and the gathering night. In the centre of it all the *Unbroken*, a small but vicious shape, belching fire and destruction!

The centre arch received hit after hit, and we hoped with each new explosion to see it crumble and collapse. But it held, although great chunks flew off, leaving gaping, jagged hollows in the brickwork. The gun banged monotonously every nine seconds. The gun's crew and ammunition party were a smooth, magnificently co-ordinated machine.

After ten minutes I decided there was no point in compromising ourselves any further. 'Cease fire!' I ordered.

'Check! Check! Check!' yelled Thirsk. 'Train fore and aft. . . . Secure the gun.'

'Stand by to dive.' I crossed to the voice-pipe. 'Half astern together. Hard-a-port.'

The ammunition party bundled down the conning-tower followed by the gun's crew. As he passed me, Fenton reported: 'Gun secured, sir. Gun empty.'

'Stop port . . . Full ahead port . . . Midships.' The boat swung to starboard. I searched the horizon to seawards, but saw nothing to break the angry western sky.

'Hard-a-starboard . . . Stop starboard . . . Full ahead starboard.' Ashore the dust and smoke wafted slowly down the valley. All was deathly quiet.

Telegraphist Morris ran a pencil down a large signal-pad. 'Sixty-eight rounds fired, sir.'

I nodded and followed him down the conning-tower hatch. With a slight shudder, the *Unbroken* dived.

In the ward-room I was joined by Thirsk and Haddow, who had recorded the shoot through the high-power periscope. Between us we assessed results. We concluded that the line must be out of action for at least twenty-four hours. A careful survey would have to be carried out before the weight of a train could be risked on it. From our own observations it was more than likely that extensive repairs would have to be made. These might take a week, or longer. If they did, no less than 100,000 tons of supplies would have been held up.

Our evening meal was a chatty, light-hearted affair. In the circumstances, we were making the best of the Christmas season – a ship sunk, the main railway line to the south blocked, and not a penn'orth of retribution. We were getting our own back. Having sunk us three times, the Germans would find we made substantial ghosts.

We spent the next three days at the entrance to the Gulf of Naples, but the only activity was in the air as transports flew Hun reinforcements to Africa.

Then, on January 1st, by way of a New Year's greeting, and to celebrate my twenty-eighth birthday, I decided to return to the viaduct and have another crack at it. But the weather was against us and I had to call it off. As we battled seawards through a rolling, crashing storm, P.O. Willey came into the ward-room with a signal. A smile wreathed his usually impassive face. 'Congratulations, sir.'

My birthday present from His Majesty the King was the award of the D.S.O.

Haddow had been given the D.S.C., Manuel a bar to his

D.S.M. Sizer, Willey and Lee, the T.G.M., were also awarded D.S.M.s Sharp, Lewis and 'Pedro' Fenton received 'Mentions'. Naturally there were disappointments. We all took the same risks, and did the same amount of work. But it was impossible that we should all be given awards, and I hoped the others would regard the decorations as gestures towards the boat as a whole. I think they did, and it was a happy, if uncomfortable, submarine that pitched and tossed on a corkscrew course back towards Malta. In the end the movements became so violent it was impossible to control the boat at a depth of less than seventy feet. Even then she rolled fifteen degrees each way, and there was a great deal of lusty cursing as men were thrown from their feet by the violence of the storm. To add to our annoyance every single item of crockery was smashed – rarer-than-gold cups and plates that Sizer had replaced after the depth-charging only by bribing the Maltese storeman with a jar of rum. We ate off the tables until January 6th when *Speedy* escorted us back into harbour, Jolly Roger flying to indicate our successes.

The high spirits of our welcome were dashed by the news that P.48, commanded by my good and old friend, Michael Faber, had been lost. It was a sad blow for Ting, too; P.48 was the boat she had launched at Barrow. The luckiest man in Malta when the news came through was the Asdic operator of the P.48. Cryer had been given a rest, and P.48 had loaned us one of their chaps to replace him.

Irritating news at Malta was that I'd missed seeing Tubby Linton. While we were operating from Gib. and Malta, he had been based at Beirut with the 1st flotilla. Transferred to the George Cross Island to increase our strength in the Central Mediterranean, he had arrived during my previous patrol and was now away on a patrol of his own. I cursed missing him, looked forward to a grand reunion when he returned to harbour, and was tickled pink at the 'bottle' he inadvertently caused the C.-in-C. to give 'Shrimp' Simpson.

Apart from food, the ward-room at Lazaretto was often

short of booze, and when 'Shrimp' heard that Tubby was coming from Beirut, he signalled Captain 'S' of the 1st flotilla: 'Please send gin and matches in *Turbulent* for a Happy Christmas.' Unfortunately the signal was intercepted by the C.-in-C.'s monitoring staff and taken to Sir Andrew Cunningham. Sir Andrew apparently disapproved of the signal channels being used in such a frivolous manner, and told 'Shrimp' so. None the less the gin and matches arrived as part of Tubby Linton's armament.

As it turned out, I never did see Tubby Linton again. Every time I was in harbour he was at sea and *vice versa*. Finally the tragic news came through that the *Turbulent* had been lost during a valiant attempt to penetrate the defences of Maddalena harbour and sink a cruiser there. With more than 90,000 tons of enemy shipping to his credit, Tubby was the most outstanding of all Mediterranean submarine commanders. His V.C., awarded posthumously, had been earned a dozen times over. His was a bitter, irreplaceable loss.

Two other submarines had arrived at Malta while we were away: the *Thunderbolt* – formerly the ill-fated *Thetis* – commanded by Lieut.-Commander 'Lucky' Crouch, and the unnamed P.311, skippered by Commander Dick Cayley.

It was as well we had taken the suckling pig, beer and plum duff to sea with us, for when we went in search of our delayed Christmas dinner, we were met with innocent eyebrow raising, expressions of shamefaced guilt, or vague apologies. However, there was an ironic twist to the gluttony. For a long time unused to large quantities of rich fare, the hogs had spent many days in bed with tortured stomachs.

As always, my first visit after handing in my patrol report was to collect mail from Ting. The usual pile awaited me. Malta had offered little opportunity for Christmas shopping, but I had managed to buy a gay tablecloth and some napkins and send them home with an England-bound submarine. Ting reported their safe arrival.

June, now ten months old, was demanding her full share of attention, and Ting, while keeping an eye on her, helped balance the family budget by knitting bed-jackets for the more elegant of Aldeburgh's pin-ups. It appeared, too, that when Ting's aunt was presented with a pheasant shot by the local soldiery, she would pay Ting two bob for the unpleasant business of plucking it! The radio provided an unusual source of revenue, for whenever my name was mentioned over it, certain of the old dears in the town insisted on presenting Ting with stamps for June's National Savings book.

I did not know it at the time – thank God! – but ten minutes after Ting wheeled June out of the post office after posting her Christmas mail to me, the building received a direct hit. The nearest she came to mentioning air raids was a light-hearted reference to the Morrison shelter installed in the back room, and I continued to thank my lucky stars that she and the child were well away from trouble.

Sad news at Malta was that 'Shrimp' Simpson was returning to England. His relief was Captain G. C. Phillips, D.S.O., who had a distinguished North Sea record in submarines. Before we made our good-byes, however, there was time for another patrol, off the North African coast.

The situation there had undergone a great change since Paul Thirsk complained the water was 'too bloody shallow'. The depth was unaltered, and the minefields were still greedy for British ships, but the Eighth Army, advancing as fast as their transport could carry them, had already reached Buratel-Sun, a thousand miles from Alamein, and were regrouping for a final thrust towards Tripoli.

The success of their advance was reflected at Malta. Air raids had died to mere token gestures, and the majority of such intruders were soon blasted from the sky by the R.A.F. The enemy could not even carry out a good reconnaissance. Food was in fairly plentiful supply, and M.T.B.s had arrived to pay back a little E-boat harrying.

There was only one shadow on this excellent state of affairs. Haig Haddow fell sick, and had to be taken to hospital. Paul Thirsk was appointed Number One, and Sub-Lieutenant J. D. Lanning, a tall, fair, vague-looking young man, came as navigator.

On January 16th we sailed. By the 19th the Eighth Army, again on the move, had captured Misurata and were closing the remaining hundred miles to Tripoli. The Germans were attempting to gather their forces for a last desperate stand behind the Mareth Line on Tunisia's southern borders. Their fleeing land transport harried with ever-increasing fury by the R.A.F., they made an all-out effort to utilise the shipping at Tripoli to hasten their retreat. This shipping was what we were after.

The *Unbroken*'s patrol position was off Ras Turgeuness, and at 4.50 on the evening of the 19th we sighted masts six miles to southwards sailing towards us. As our quarry approached, we identified the 6,000-ton troopship, *Edda*. A torpedo attack was almost unnecessary. She was so laden with troops that her gunwales were awash, and it seemed as though a heavy sea would swamp her. A magnificent target.

She was escorted by two torpedo-boats, and Cryer reported that both had Asdics switched on. Beyond the torpedo-boats, as an added escort, were three schooners. Still vividly haunted by memories of the past, we quickly shut off for depth-charging, for we did not want to join the masses of oily flotsam that littered the area.

Silently we waited as the convoy drew nearer. We adjusted our own position for the attack. The trooper was doing eight knots, and I let her have a salvo of four kippers from a range of fifteen hundred yards.

Then we went down, but not too far down, for the water was only a hundred feet deep. We stopped at seventy – and waited. To our delight there was a shattering detonation as one torpedo struck home.

Then, to my dismay, I heard the familiar noise of a propeller – but without the accompanying express train! It zinged right over the top of the control-room.

What in God's name is this?

Manuel, still the most experienced of us, whispered in my ear: 'It's a torpedo, sir. It's circling.'

I felt the sweat jump from my forehead. *Hell and damnation, we're going to kipper ourselves! The damned thing's gone wrong somewhere.* . . . I felt a moment of rage towards Lee and his torpedo-men. Then I rebuked myself for being unfair. This was only the second defect in nearly forty torpedoes fired, and in any case some of the torpedoes weren't so hot on arrival from the makers. A second *zzzzing* brought me back to the immediate urgency of the moment.

Instinctively we all ducked. The top of the bridge structure was only fifty feet below the surface and the lunatic torpedo might well be running at that depth by now. It sounded close enough.

Again it came circling round. There was no doubt about it: one more crazy sweep and the damn thing would blow us to shattering destruction. The sound of its propeller faded into the distance, then came rushing back. Louder... louder . . . louder . . . until, by a miracle – and what else could it have been? – the wretched brute shot down past us to bury its nose in the mud of the ocean floor.

Before a shivering reaction set in the first depth charges came down. But they came singly, and a long way off. There were only seven of them. The runaway torpedo had also struck the fear of God into the enemy. Ten minutes after the last ashcan exploded in the distance I ordered a return to periscope depth.

One of the torpedo-boats was still hunting us, but was a good way off. The second was standing by the *Edda*, taking survivors aboard. The schooners were well out of the picture. The *Edda* was sinking stern first. An ant swarm of men slithered over her side into the unfriendly sea. Satisfied, we slipped down again, and returned to periscope depth six minutes later for a final look. The *Edda* had sunk. Despite the lunatic torpedo it had been an easy kill.

Soon it was sunset, and when we surfaced we observed flares and flak from the position of our attack. The R.A.F. were on the job, finishing off the torpedo-boats. I learned later that they claimed the *Edda*, too, but I convinced them that Mussolini's daughter was ours for ever.

The remainder of the patrol was uneventful save for the sighting of 'F' boats – enemy landing-craft heavily armed with anti-aircraft guns. As many as a dozen of these guns were of a type similar to the British Bofors, making an 'F' boat a serious menace to a surfaced submarine. A submarine could not use torpedoes against them because of their shallow draught, and in a gun battle one 3-inch gun was useless against a massed salvo of Bofors.

As most of the enemy's larger vessels had been sunk or had fled the scene, our continued presence in the area was considered unnecessary. After seven days at sea we were recalled to Malta to take part in another special operation.

We were met by the minesweeper *Hebe* at the entrance to the searched channel, and as we moved into harbour the cruisers *Euryalus* and *Cleopatra*, escorted by four destroyers, swept past into Grand Harbour. Our Jolly Roger, signifying the success of the patrol, fluttered saucily from the mast, and as the towering monsters crashed by me I felt a resurgence of all the old pride of being a sub-mariner.

On arrival I made a verbal report to 'Shrimp' of the *Edda* sinking, then brought up the question of the *Unbroken*'s return to England. We had been away eleven months, and I reminded 'Shrimp' of the danger of growing stale. I pointed out that more than one submarine had been lost because of staleness – or because success had developed into reckless cockiness – and I assured 'Shrimp' that I wanted neither of these things to happen to the *Unbroken*. I added that I was good for perhaps four more patrols, but could not guarantee my nerves and strength beyond that. I concluded by saying that the Admiralty seemed to make no move to recall submarines from the Med. after they had done a year there, and that our year was nearly completed.

'No one laid down that a year was the maximum time for a submarine to be away', said 'Shrimp'.

'I know, sir,' I replied, 'but I give a year as the maximum for the simple reason that a submarine that doesn't get out after a year *never* gets out.'

'Shrimp' nodded and said he would do his best. I knew he meant what he said, and I forgot my sorrows by getting well and truly plastered at his farewell party.

Then came the business of preparing for our next operation. A visit to Lascaris put me in the picture.

The Eighth Army had reached Tripoli and was advancing towards the Mareth Line. The bulk of the enemy's supplies were coming through the northern ports of Bizerta and Tunis, and the main railway line from these ports ran across the Cape Bon peninsula, down to Hammamet by the sea, then south along the Gulf of Hammamet keeping two or three miles inland. Near Bou Ficha the line crossed a high, vulnerable viaduct. Its destruction would cut Rommel's main supply line in half.

The Germans were well aware of this, and had surrounded the viaduct with so many ack-ack guns the valley bristled like a porcupine. All allied attempts to bomb the viaduct had failed.

A new scheme had been evolved: eight commandos would land from the sea and attempt to blow up the viaduct. The *Unbroken* would take them there and, it was hoped, bring them back.

In general charge was thin, aquiline Commander D. H. Fyffe, D.S.C., R.N.R., a submarine veteran of the First World War. Having trained the commandos for the job he proposed to come with us to see everything went according to plan. In charge of the landing-party was short, wiry Captain J. Eyre of the Royal Engineers, with Lieutenant P. M. Thomas of the Buffs as his second in command: a tough-looking young man who seemed a typical 'regular army' type. The remaining six in the party were Fighting Frenchmen.

They brought aboard four folboats and enormous quantities of arms and explosives which, after being landed on the beach, they would have to haul over two-and-a-half miles of rough, heavily defended country. While Thirsk visited the hospital to see Haddow – alas, he was still too sick to rejoin us – I kept a watchful eye on the explosives, for I wanted to be certain they did not embark any of Peter Churchill's 'pressurised pencils'.

At tea-time on January 25th we cast off and proceeded from the harbour. I asked the two army officers to go below, but they stayed put on the bridge, anxious to miss nothing of the novelty of being aboard a submarine. I didn't press the point: they had enough troubles ahead of them without my spoiling their fun 'rubbernecking'.

Commander Fyffe, full of nostalgia for the old days, was soon at home, billeted in the spare bunk in the ward-room. The two army officers were squeezed into the petty officers' mess, while the Frenchmen were bundled for'ard. They seemed very lost and unhappy in their new surroundings, but our boys did their best to make them feel at home, large gulps of rum and sign language compensating for their inability to speak French.

On the morning of January 27th we dived into the Gulf of Hammamet to test the currents, for it was most important the commandos should be landed at the nearest point on the beach to their objective. Through the periscope the town of Hammamet looked tired, sunbaked, empty and lazy; a cluster of white, low-roofed buildings dried up by the desert sun. As I swept the shore towards Bou Ficha where the commandos were to be disembarked, however, the scene changed. The road was alive with heavy traffic moving south. The beach was filled with patrols, marching singly with bayonets fixed, or driving backwards and forwards in lorries and open trucks. The chances against our mission succeeding seemed heavy. I ordered a withdrawal from the gulf, handed the periscope to Archdale who was officer of the watch, and crossed unhappily to the ward-room.

I had not been there ten minutes when an embarrassed Archdale entered and said: 'Bit awkward, sir. Commander Fyffe says he's taken over. Told me to carry on.'

'The devil he has,' I muttered, and hurried to the control room. Fyffe was studying the shore through the high-power periscope, seemingly oblivious to any danger that might sweep in from the sky. Quickly I crossed to the after periscope, ordered it to be raised and scanned the blue, cloudless heavens. Fortunately they were empty.

Fyffe looked across at me quizzically. 'Everything's in hand,' he assured me.

I was reluctant to hurt his feelings by telling him that submarine warfare had altered considerably in the past quarter of a century, but I told him, quite firmly, that my watchkeeping officers were capable of doing their jobs.

He looked crestfallen. 'I only wanted to give the boys a rest,' he assured me.

I smiled, and there were apologies all round. Things returned to normal – Ted Archdale in charge.

Captain Eyre and Lieutenant Thomas had a long look at the shore through the periscope and joined me in the ward-room. They said nothing, but I could tell they were as unhappy about the situation as I was. Rather than brood over it, however, we went over the details of the landing.

'We'll run out now,' I said, 'and surface after dusk. Then we'll turn around and come back towards your landing-point. On the way in the folboats will be taken on deck ready for launching. I'll take you to within a mile of the beach, stop, and launch all four boats together. We'll give you a course to steer that will take you exactly to the chosen spot. Then it's up to you.'

Captain Eyre nodded. 'Good. We'll keep all four boats together. After striking the beach they'll be hauled up near the water's edge and turned round ready for a quick rush to the water. Then we'll make inland with the explosives.'

'If any alarm is given,' I said, 'and we have to clear out, I'll let you know what's happening by firing two star shells in the direction of Hammamet. If you don't see a star shell we'll still be waiting for you.'

Thomas grinned. 'If we see a star shell, that's when we start becoming Frenchmen, eh?'

I grinned back, hoping I concealed the heaviness that lay over my heart.

At 5.30 p.m. we ran out, waited until darkness before surfacing. We turned about and crept towards land on our almost inaudible motors. A light off-shore breeze set tiny waves lapping against the bows, the gun's crew closed up, a double set of look-outs peered anxiously into the night. At full buoyancy the folboats were dragged through the fore hatch. We trimmed down to reduce silhouette and closed the beach along the prepared line of soundings. Not a word was spoken save for the whispered passing of orders, but I could hear, more expressive than speech, the sharp, nervous breathing of all those crowded on the bridge. A mile from shore the motors were stopped.

The black-out ashore was broken with sickening regularity by the headlights of motor convoys racing down the road to the south. The commandos would have to cross this road with their explosives.

The *Unbroken* drifted to a standstill, her bows pointing towards the still and silent beach of Hammamet. I leaned over the bridge and whispered to Archdale: 'Launch the boats quietly, keep them secured alongside and get the men embarked.'

'Aye, aye, sir.'

Commander Fyffe went for'ard to the casing to help the Frenchmen into their boats. 'So long, and good luck,' he said.

My God, if anyone needs luck, they do.

From Archdale: 'All ready now, sir.'

'All right.' The two army officers moved for'ard. Silently they shook hands with me, then clambered down to the casing. 'God speed,' I murmured. To Archdale: 'Tell Commander Fyffe to send them in.'

'Aye, aye, sir.'

A minute later they disappeared into the night.

'Half astern together.'

WE withdrew a few cables, then turned slowly round. Our bows pointed seawards. Fyffe rejoined me on the bridge. We kept our glasses trained towards land, saying nothing, but sharing a common agony of fear for the men paddling towards the shore.

Seven-forty-five. By now they would be on the beach. The minutes dragged by.

At eight o'clock I jumped with alarm as three single tracer shots were fired in the air over Hammamet.

Silence again.

A file of lorries rumbled through the night towards the battlefront.

Restless, one of the look-outs shifted on his feet and muttered to himself. I lowered my glasses and rubbed a hand across my eyes. 'Reckon they must be well on their way.'

'They've been ashore nearly an hour,' Fyffe replied. 'Must be a good way inland by now.'

'I suppose we'll hear the bang.'

'Quite a time to go, yet.'

At that moment there were three small explosions and a flash from just beyond the beach.

'Damnation, I don't like that. What do you think they were? Grenades?'

Fyffe sighed. 'Might be. That or small mines.'

The party were armed with grenades, and if they had used them, or had set off mines, the game was up.

And then, as though by a prearranged signal, a row of flares suddenly illuminated the entire beach. No men were in sight, but in the centre of the brilliant, dazzling light were four folboats, neatly lined up a few feet from the water.

The bridge of the submarine was illuminated so plainly I could see every detail of Fyffe's drawn face as he gazed intently at the shore, his brows furrowed, his eyes wrinkled. I remembered my words to Peter Churchill: *You can see them, but they can't see you,* but I knew that it was but a matter of minutes before flares were fired over the sea.

In any case the folboats were exposed and the commandos could never return to the *Unbroken*.

I turned to Fyffe, sick at heart. 'What else can we do?'

'Nothing.' His voice was flat and empty. 'I think it's all over. Have they seen the submarine?'

'Not yet. . . . Do you agree we should go?'

'Yes. No point sticking our necks out further.'

I took a last look at the shore. The scene was unchanged as flare after flare blazed in the sky revealing the four folboats on the bare African beach. I turned to the voice-pipe. 'Full ahead together . . . Starboard twenty. Steer one-five-six. Start the engines.' The boat leapt to life. I leaned over to the gun's crew. 'With star shell, *load*! On bearing red one-five-oh, at maximum elevation, fire two rounds independently.' Back to the voice-pipe. 'Control-room. Broadcast that we are firing star shell to indicate to the commandos our withdrawal. The alarm has been raised.'

The flares from our shells hung like candelabras in the sky before they drifted slowly to earth, dimming as they floated down, sharing our sadness.

'Clear the casing.'

The words were hardly out of my mouth when the starboard look-out roared: 'Object bearing green five-oh!'

'Klaxon! Klaxon!'

The alarm signal screamed through the boat.

Fyffe bundled through the hatch like an expert, once again feeling the old thrill. I followed, and we rattled down to seventy feet.

'Fast H.E. bearing green four-oh.'

'Group down. Half ahead together.'

I grabbed the earphones. *Fast diesel engines. No 'pinging'. Probably 'F' boats. Had we stayed on the surface another minute they would have blown us to pieces. . . .*

An hour later we surfaced to see that flares continued to turn the night over Bou Ficha into day. The hunt was still on.

Reluctantly we headed for Malta. The Commandos were never heard of again.

Our return was sad and silent. Often on the bridge I would find myself involuntarily looking over my shoulder as though expecting folboats from the direction of Bou Ficha. Although I knew there was nothing we could have done but leave when we did, I was glad the responsibility for withdrawing had not been mine. This is no reflection on Commander Fyffe; an admission, rather, of my own relief at not having had to make the heart-breaking decision. Consequently, when Fyffe asked if he might join our 'watch-keepers' union', I readily consented, for there is little opportunity for self-searching and recrimination when you are engaged in a periscope sweep of hostile sky and ocean.

Our arrival at Lazaretto was brightened by the reappearance of Haddow, but he came only to say good-bye. He was off home to take his Command course. I was pleased he was in line for his own boat, yet I was sorry to see him go, for his departure meant the loss of a good, trusted friend as well as a fine officer. In the months we had spent together a great intimacy had developed between us, based not so much upon words as upon a deep, common understanding.

Thirsk stayed on as first lieutenant, while Sub-Lieutenant Evatt, son of the Australian statesman, came aboard to relieve Lanning as navigator. He was an extremely efficient young man: tough-looking and dark, very certain of himself, surprisingly undemonstrative for an Aussie. He was only temporary, however, and after two patrols was replaced by B. S. Richards, M.B.E., R.N.V.R., a short, dark sub-lieutenant aged about twenty-four.

Sizer, Willey, Bramhall and a few of the others were given a rest from the next two patrols – dull, uneventful affairs – and on one of them we took with us the *Unbroken*'s next captain: Bevis Andrew, D.S.C., a slim, tall, dark lieutenant addicted to wing collars. It had been decided that although the *Unbroken* was not to return to England until September, I was to fly back in April.

I was beset with conflicting emotions at the news. On the one hand I was glad to be going home. Apart from the physical strain, my nerves were beginning to fray after a year of submarine warfare in the Med. Naturally, I was overjoyed at the thought of returning to Ting and the daughter I had never seen. On the other hand, though, I felt guilty at having to leave behind the officers and men of my crew. They, too, had suffered their share of physical strain and mental stress. They, too, had wives and sweethearts awaiting them. We had come out as one tight-knit unit and I felt we should stay that way until the end. If I went back, we should all go back. It had not been just for myself that I'd raised with 'Shrimp' the matter of our recall. But My Lords at the Admiralty had made a decision, and there was nothing I could do save lament it.

Unlike the Staff Officers at Whitehall, most of whom had never seen the inside of a submarine, I knew only too well the danger of staleness that resulted from a too-long commission. The success and survival of a submarine depends upon the sharp, keen, nerve-taut efficiency of every single member of her crew. It is an efficiency that does not apply to battleships and cruisers, for aboard one of those giants an entire gun's crew can grow slack and stale without appreciably lowering the overall efficiency of the ship. In a submarine, however, the dulled reflexes of one man can mean disaster. That was what I meant when I told 'Shrimp' that a submarine that did not return home after twelve months in the Med. *never* returned. I am certain that 'Shrimp', as a sub-mariner, must have agreed with me, but he was just a four-ringed captain at the time and was able to do no more than make formally worded 'recommendations'.

One 'S' boat and seven 'T' boats had been lost, including Tubby Linton's *Turbulent*. Ten lost – counting *Utmost* and P.48 – and many narrow escapes. Soon to go were the *Regent, Splendid, Sahib* and *Saracen*. The new P.51, for instance had taken a terrible pounding that caused her to dive to three-hundred-and-sixty feet – twice her designed depth – while Dickie Gatehouse in an 'S' boat was cruelly savaged by an Allied pilot who failed to read his orders properly.

With memories of these gallant comrades running through my mind I set sail from Malta on March 26th, 1943; my twelfth and last patrol as Captain of the *Unbroken*. Our orders were to make for the Cape Spartivento-Cretone area to harass enemy shipping en route for Tunis.

We reached Cretone on March 31st and through the periscope I recognised the landmarks of the ill-fated 'Tug' Wilson operation: the chemical factory belching heavy smoke; the surrounding countryside, fresh and green; the sharp whiteness of the anti-submarine schooners. The night was clear with a cool off-shore breeze. At ten o'clock I huddled into my deck-chair, wished Archdale a quiet watch and closed my eyes.

Perhaps five minutes later I was awakened by Ted's urgent whisper: 'Captain, sir.'

I jumped up. Archdale pointed. 'Bow-wave, sir.'

I levelled my glasses. A lean, low phosphorescence not far away. *A U-boat coming from Taranto*. I leaned over the voice-pipe. 'Night alarm!' Our bows leapt forward as the motors automatically went to half-ahead.

The enemy was moving fast from port to starboard. It

would be thirty seconds before the tubes were reported ready.

'Ship's head?'

From the voice-pipe: 'Oh-seven-oh, sir.'

'Starboard twenty. Steer one-one-oh.'

As the bows swung to starboard I set the torpedo night sight for an enemy speed of fifteen knots. I was about to pass a firing interval below when Archdale grasped my arm. 'It's not a U-boat, sir,' he cried. 'It's a bloody E-boat or a submarine-chaser.'

He was right. The lean shape had resolved itself into a fast surface vessel with a wicked-looking gun in her bows.

'Klaxon! Klaxon! . . . Eighty feet!' I shut the voice-pipe cock. The spray from the vents shot upwards. I turned towards the conning-tower hatch. Archdale was crouched over it.

'Why the hell aren't you below?'

'Some hold-up in the conning-tower, sir.'

'What the blazes is going on down there?' I roared.

'Can't get down, sir,' shouted a look-out.

We were diving fast. The water was swirling round the gun.

I gave Archdale a push. 'Stand on his bloody head.'

He did so, and the cursing chain of men in the conning-tower collapsed into the control-room. Archdale climbed into the conning-tower. Another jam.

The sea rushed through the clearing ports at the sides of the bridge. I jumped on Archdale's shoulders and pushed. With a crash and a clatter he tumbled into the control-room and I found myself hanging with one hand to the ladder, the upper hatch open above my head. I hauled myself up, grabbed the lid, pulled it down and rammed home a clip.

'One clip on!' I yelled. If the men in the control-room thought the upper hatch still open they would have shut the lower one and left me trapped in the conning-tower. I put on the other clip, inserted the locking-pins and slithered down the ladder. My head and neck were dripping with water. The sea had caught up with me as I pulled the hatch down.

Osborne shut the lower lid. In the dull red light of the control-room I could see the depth gauges already showed forty feet. I turned to Thirsk. 'Blow "Q" at sixty-five, then flatten-out at eighty. There's a sub-chaser on top. May have seen us or heard the klaxon.'

I looked down and saw our Bren gun – a recent addition to the armament – lying on the control-room deck. 'Manuel! What's this doing here, and what happened in the conning-tower?'

Self-consciously he explained.

I had approved that Cryer should be Bren operator at gun action stations. Consequently, when 'Night Alarm' was sounded he handed the Asdic to Jones, grabbed the Bren and his home-made canvas bandolier containing spare clips, and closed-up at the foot of the conning-tower with the gun's crew.

Suddenly an imp of the perverse crept into him and he decided he ought to be by my side.

'Permission to go on the bridge, sir?' he asked Thirsk.

'No,' said Paul, 'you might not be needed.'

'I'm going up anyway,' he announced.

'You're not.'

'Oh yes I am.' And with that he started to climb the conning-tower. It was then the klaxon sounded – hence the conning-tower blockage. Paul Thirsk grabbed Cryer's ankles and that, plus the pressure from above, sent the burly six-footer crashing back into the control-room. . . .

I listened to Manuel's story and scratched my chin.

'Where's Cryer now?'

'By the time you got down, sir, the first lieutenant had put him under arrest. He's for'ard in the torpedo compartment.'

I grunted. 'Tell Petty Officer Lee to keep him there until I decide what's to be done.'

'Aye, aye, sir.'

At this point Micky Jones picked up our enemy. By some freak of good fortune she had not seen us and was continuing on her course as though nothing had happened.

When the panic died down we surfaced and set course for Cap del Armi, Cryer locked up for'ard.

On the afternoon of April 3rd an unescorted warship hove in sight making for the Straits of Messina at speed. As we started an attack we found it difficult to identify her. I thought she might be a cruiser of the new, small *Regolo* class, but that was pure guesswork since we knew no more about these ships than the fact that they displaced some 5,000 tons. Then, as I swept the sky, I saw she had considerable air protection. I was puzzled that a ship of her size should have aircraft cover yet no surface escort, but decided to postpone further speculation until after we had sunk her.

The attack was a long-range affair, and we fired a salvo of four torpedoes from a position far on her starboard quarter. We went deep to avoid the aircraft, and at the right time heard two explosions. Somehow they did not sound very convincing, but when we crept back to periscope depth we saw only the aircraft, and thought she might indeed have been sunk. Later, however, we discovered our target – the enemy's crack anti-submarine vessel: a converted warship captured from the Greeks – was still in one piece. She had already sunk one British submarine and had nearly finished off another. I was pleased to have had a shot at her, sorry to have missed, and more than grateful not to have known at the time what I was tackling!

The next day we were haunted by aircraft patrols. Their attentions became so persistent I wondered whether the enemy had evolved a method of detecting submerged submarines from the air. In the early part of the afternoon we went down to ninety feet out of their way.

I was in the ward-room when Petty Officer Lee arrived to say: 'Cryer says he can hear Asdic impulses.'

I frowned. 'I thought he was for'ard in the torpedo compartment?'

'He is, sir.'

'Do you mean to tell me he can hear supersonic Asdic waves without a set?'

'He says he can hear them, sir.'

I hurried to the control-room. 'Hear anything on the Asdic?'

'No, sir.'

Cryer's gone round the bend. . . . Maybe there's a defect on the set. . . . But surely Cryer can't hear Asdic impulses with the naked ear? . . .

I turned to Lee. 'Cryer. Do you think he's mad?'

'Looks all right, sir.'

'No wild eyes or waving arms?'

'No, sir.'

Richards was officer of the watch. 'Bring her up,' I said. 'Twenty-six feet. . . .'

As we tilted upwards there was a shout from Jones on the Asdic: 'H.E. red one-two-oh.'

Cryer was right!

'Diving stations!'

I trained the periscope on the bearing of the H.E., and as the glass broke the surface I gasped. 'It's the biggest bloody tanker you've ever seen!' She was a mile away and as I swung the periscope I saw she was escorted by three destroyers and a number of aircraft.

'Bearing now?'

'Red one-three-oh.'

'Range now?'

'Two thousand five hundred.'

'Start the attack. Bring all tubes to the ready. Hard a-starboard. Group up. . . . Full ahead together.'

As the periscope slid back into its well I had a last look before firing – if there would be time to fire at all. 'We've got three minutes', I announced. 'Go down to forty feet on the turn, but I must be back at twenty-six feet in two minutes.' I was seventy degrees on her port bow. 'Give me a course for a track angle of a hundred-and-twenty degrees.'

The boat shuddered as the propellers lashed the water at their top speed. The *Unbroken* spun like a top to starboard. Excited at the thought of a 10,000-ton tanker, I forgot her escorting destroyers.

'Two minutes at full group up, sir.'

'Group down.' I turned to Thirsk. 'Go to half group down when you can. Remember that I've got to see what I'm doing.' He nodded.

'All tubes ready.'

'Stand by. . . . Up after periscope.'

As the periscope slid up I whispered to Manuel: 'Fix me on the D.A. as soon as I can see. . . . Are you steady on your course?'

'Not quite, sir. Ten degrees to go.'

I could see now. I twisted the periscope against Manuel's chest. 'Re-set.'

'On now.' His breath was hot against the back of my neck.

'Leave ten degrees of starboard wheel on. Let her swing.'

'Aye, aye, sir.'

The cross-wire of the periscope was a quarter of a length ahead of the tanker.

'Fire One.'

The boat rebounded.

'Torpedo running.'

The tanker's bows touched the cross-wire. 'Fire Two.'

Again the rebound and pressure on the ears as the air was vented back into the boat from the empty tube. 'Fire Three.'

The tanker's stern crept to the cross-wire. 'Fire Four.'

'All torpedoes running.'

I pressed the klaxon. 'Q' flooded with a rush of air and we went deep. Five minutes had passed since 'Diving stations.'

There was a shattering explosion.

'We've hit her!' A delighted cheer filled the boat.

'Eighty feet. Shut-off for depth-charging. . . . Group

down. Starboard fifteen, steer east. . . . Silent routine.'

I relaxed – and remembered. 'Tell Cryer to come and man the Asdic.' A moment later he bounded aft, grinning all over his face.

The enemy were soon on to us. They dropped thirty-five charges, but none sounded dangerously close. Then they turned back to the crippled tanker and surrounded her against a second attack. We returned to periscope depth for a look. The weather had closed in, but I could see a great cloud of smoke towards the shore. We returned to the depths and a little later heard a long rumbling explosion.

'I hope she's blown up,' said Thirsk.

His hopes were justified. It was later confirmed she had gone down. A delightful farewell gesture to the Med. To save face the enemy claimed for the fourth time that the *Unbroken* had also been sunk.

When we surfaced that night we were astounded to see that the bridge had suffered considerable damage during the depth-charge attack. The night sights had been smashed, the framework of the bridge was buckled and crumpled, and the glass of the navigation lights, designed to withstand pressure six hundred feet down, was shattered. Yet none of us in the control-room had been aware of the nearness of the depth charges. The Powers that Be could say what they liked, but the fact remained that we were getting stale. Yet I was the only one going home. To sharpen the boys up a little I gave them a full quota of exercises on the journey back to Malta: practice attacks, emergency increases in depth, gun action stations and change-round exercises.

Dawn of April 7th would see us at the entrance to the searched channel. After we surfaced on the evening of the 6th I began packing my gear. It is strange, but from the moment of starting on that patrol, right until the moment I embarked upon an aircraft for Gib., I was quite unexcited at the thought of going home. Instead I was oppressed by unhappiness at leaving the *Unbroken*, for it is not easy to tear yourself away from a bunch of good, decent men with whom you have lived for seventeen months, and with whom you might well have died.

After our evening meal glasses were raised to wish each other 'Good luck', and later, when we were alone, I yarned with Thirsk over the times we had spent together. . . . Our arrival at Barrow in all the gloom of a Lancashire winter. . . . Trials at Arrochar. . . . The incident with the British ship en route to Gib. . . . Peter Churchill and his desperadoes. . . . Our first heart-cheering kill. . . . The 'Italian' schooner. . . . The minefields to Malta and our greatest moment when we crippled the two cruisers. . . . Bombarding the railways and Operation Folboat. . . . The murderous depth-charging that nearly finished us off and the torpedo that went mad off the African coast. . . . The sinking of the *Edda* and the abortive attempt on the viaduct. . . .

Before climbing to my deck-chair on the bridge I listened for a moment to all the old familiar sounds and found it difficult to believe I was hearing them for the last time. I would doubtless command other submarines, but every boat has its own peculiar individuality, indefinable but very real, and the *Unbroken*, despite her cold steel bulk, had her own special voice and personality. Aboard her I had sailed more than 24,000 miles, suffered about 400 depth charges around my ears, sunk more than 30,000 tons of shipping, and crippled two cruisers. During our twelve patrols we had spent 210 days at sea, and the hours submerged totalled 100 of them. I had fired forty-five torpedoes, and had taken part in four special operations and many gun actions. It was not a bad record. . . .

Andrew came aboard at Malta and I introduced him to the crew as they stood gathered on the casing. I scanned their familiar faces and a lump came to my throat. Thirsk, Archdale; Sizer, imperturbable as granite; Manuel, wise and confident. 'Pedro' Fenton, the gunlayer, and his pal, the irrepressible Jan Cryer. Butterworth, looking as hard-done-by as ever; 'Trampy' Mullet badly in need of a hair-cut. Lee, Scutt, Jones, McTeare and the rest – fine, good men every one; as hand-picked a crew as any submarine commander could wish for.

I don't think what I said to them made very much sense. I cannot remember it now, nor could I five minutes after the speech was made. I know I thanked them for all they had done, and made one or two not very funny jokes. But it was all very misty and unreal and sad. There were handshakes and cheers and cries of: 'Good luck, sir,' and when I walked ashore the slow drag of my feet was due to more than a cramped fortnight on patrol.

There was a party in the Lazaretto ward-room, and on April 12th Thirsk came to Halfia aerodrome to see me off. As my Dakota climbed towards the clouds I saw him, still waving, alone on the runway. We circled and turned towards Gib. I looked down and caught a last glimpse of the *Unbroken*: a slim blue matchstick twinkling in the brilliant sunlight of the Mediterranean noon.

I HAD to wait at Gib. for eleven exasperating days before I sailed home aboard the *Stirling Castle*, a troopship that formed part of a fast, England-bound convoy. It was an odd sensation, travelling on the surface both by day and by night, and as a passenger. It took a lot of getting used to.

From Liverpool I sent Ting a telegram announcing my safe arrival, and the journey from that grey, ugly seaport to Saxmundham seemed longer than any I had known. I was out of the train before it stopped, and there on the platform, bathed in the sunlight of a fine May afternoon, stood Ting – a glass of whisky held aloft in each hand. To the amusement of the other travellers, we drank each other's health there and then before a rattling, ancient taxi took us the bumping, jolting eight miles to Aldeburgh. There were a thousand things to talk about, and ten thousand others impossible to express. Perhaps the greatest delight of all was to open the cottage door and see my fifteen-months-old daughter lurching about the sitting-room. I was somewhat disconcerted, however, when she took one look at me and started to bawl her head off. After a while she came to accept me, dissolving into tears only when she felt she was not receiving her fair share of attention.

Dusk set the sirens a-wailing, and I realised for the first time that Aldeburgh was not the quiet fishing and residential town of my imagination. It had been badly bombed, had been shot-up by German fighters, and was along the route taken by the enemy when he blitzed London.

My six weeks' leave passed far too quickly, and when it was over I travelled to Northways, the headquarters of the Flag Officer (Submarines) in London, to discover what was to become of me. They told me to go out to grass for a couple of months and they would give me a tinkle when I was needed. That suited me down to the ground, and back I went to Aldeburgh to laze in the sun of the war's fourth summer.

The *Unbroken* was never far from my thoughts. For a long time I was reluctant to open a newspaper or listen to the B.B.C.s news bulletins, but although the *Saracen* and *Parthian* were included among the smooth, professionally sympathetic announcements of regret, there was no mention of the *Unbroken*.

The complete occupation of Tunisia was accompanied by the surrender of 200,000 prisoners and the capture of twenty-six German generals, including von Arnim. Sicily and Italy were invaded, and Mussolini's 'resignation' was soon to be followed by Italy's surrender. Malta came into the news again when the King, visiting North Africa, crossed to the Island aboard the cruiser *Aurora*. Mr Churchill had talks with President Roosevelt; thousand-bomber raids by the R.A.F. were almost nightly occurrences. Guy Gibson led his famous dam-busting raid. From Burma and the Pacific the news was still unhappy, but the Russians reported the wholesale decimation of the German armies on the Eastern front, and the people of Britain knew the tide had well and truly turned.

In August I felt I ought to be getting back into the war again. A second visit to Northways resulted in a Staff job with the Admiral (Submarines) in London. A desk job did not appeal to me at all, and I told them so. I was assured the post was purely temporary, and that soon I would be given another submarine. I had not been wielding my pen for many days when good news arrived: the *Unbroken* was on her way home, and would I like to meet her at H.M.S. *Dolphin*, the submarine base at Gosport? Would I like to? I was thrilled beyond words!

As I was preparing for the journey a message was handed to me. Puzzled and a little worried, I tore it open. It was a note of congratulations from the Flag Officer (Submarines) on my being awarded the D.S.C. Thirsk and Archdale had also been awarded D.S.C.s, while the D.S.M. went to Stoker P.O. Sharp, E.R.A. Lewis, Leading Stoker Fall, the ebullient Jan Cryer, and A.B. Bramhall. Mentioned in Dispatches were Lieutenant Andrew, Sub-Lieutenant Richards, Scutt – now an acting P.O. – E.R.A. Leech and P.O. Willey. Again names had been omitted – but that's the way these things happen.

I stood among wives, sweethearts and parents on the jetty as the *Unbroken* sailed into view: tired-looking and a little rusty now; not so slick as on the day when she had sailed from England; but as cocky and proud as ever – White Ensign taut in the wind, ratings correctly stiff, the skull of the Jolly Roger grinning its message of triumphant success. I glanced at the womenfolk around me: some smiling, others cheering, a few wiping tears of joyful relief from their eyes. I remembered how worried and uncertain they had been at Barrow, and I wanted to grasp their arms and say: 'I told you they'd be all right, didn't I?'

The *Unbroken* was secured, and the ratings poured ashore. Press photographers and reporters squeezed through the embracing crowd, and amid cheers and laughter I was photographed shaking hands with Andrew – resplendent, as ever, in a wing collar. I climbed aboard, and the months between disappeared as I trod her familiar bridge, surveyed the happy faces, wrinkled my nose at the oily, heavy smell that came from the conning-tower. I climbed down the ladder and crossed the control-room into the ward-room. Nothing had changed. Andrew, Archdale, Manuel, Lee and Sizer followed me in. There were congratulations and handshakes, slaps on the back and much laughter. One face was missing.

'Where's Paul Thirsk?'

'We thought you might have seen him,' said Andrew. 'He's here in England taking a Command course. He left soon after you did.'

'No, I haven't seen him. . . . And what's been happening to you?'

The day's tot had been saved, including an extra one for me, and as Sizer poured them out, I heard of the *Unbroken*'s adventures since I had left her. On his first patrol Andrew had bad luck with an Italian U-boat. After a good attack they thought they saw a torpedo hit, but the U-boat sailed right through the smoke and splash. The kipper had probably exploded prematurely. They then went close inshore on the north coast of Sicily to sink a schooner, and the highlight of subsequent patrols was a possible hit on a medium-sized supply ship. Selfishly, perhaps, I was less excited about these exploits than I was to see the *Unbroken* back home without damage or casualties, and I felt genuinely miserable when the yarning and reminiscing were over and it was time to return to London.

I tried, as well as I was able, to keep in touch with the officers and crew of the *Unbroken*, but it was not an easy task. You cannot live for ever in the past, and time dims the sincerity of solemn sworn promises. You develop new friends, new interests, new passions. The fervid reality of today becomes tomorrow's nostalgia.

With tragic irony, John Haig Haddow survived the submarine war only to be killed in a flying accident. Paul Thirsk joined the Colonial Service and until recently was secretary to the Governor of Nigeria at Lagos. Ted Archdale's real passion was gunnery and at the time of writing he is gunnery officer of a destroyer squadron in the Med., surveying a more peaceful Malta scene than the one we had known together. Chief E.R.A. Manuel left the Service and is back in his native Ireland where he works for a firm of whisky distillers. Joe Sizer, still a bachelor, is with the Royal Naval Recruiting Depôt at Manchester. Jan Cryer remains a sub-mariner, as does Petty Officer Sharp. Morgan, Willey and Lee are civilians now. So, too, are Johnny Crutch, who emigrated to Australia; Howard Lewis who is a mining engineer on the Gold Coast; 'Pedro' Fenton who was last heard of with the Birkenhead Ferry; and Scutt who is with a firm of engineers in the Persian Gulf. As for myself, I assumed command of the submarine *Thule* in December, '43, took her to the Pacific in September, '44, returning home in October, '45. I had a variety of posts before leaving the Service in June, 1952.

The *Unbroken* was handed to the Russians in 1944, together with her sister ships, *Ursula* and *Unison*, and the battleship, *Royal Sovereign*. They returned in February, 1949, and although the *Unbroken* had survived the heat of the Med. and the cold of the Arctic, had defied depth-charging, bombs and mines, she could not withstand the hammers and acetylene torches of the Newcastle scrap-yard. In 1950 she was towed there and broken up. Perhaps it was better that way. As Tennyson said of the aged Ulysses:

> How dull it is to pause, to make an end,
> To rust unburnished, not to shine in use!
> As tho' to breathe were life.

It was thus fitting that the *Unbroken*, rather than gather slime and barnacles while rotting aged and forgotten alongside some cheerless depôt ship, should have given her hard, unyielding steel back into her mother's womb to be reforged and revitalised into a new shining strength. I like to think that the *Unbroken*, in some new shape and form, continues to sail beneath the Mediterranean's blue waters, still of service to her country and the White Ensign.

London, 1952.

THE END

THE SAVAGE MOUNTAIN by WILLIE HEINRICH

Three German soldiers hole up in a tiny Czech village, the suspected headquarters of the partisans. They pretend to be deserters – but each one has his own pattern for survival, each one lives in the constant awareness that some time will come the crushing degradation of complete physical and moral defeat, the frightful havoc of a once-powerful army crushed and battered into the mud – and the terrible moment that would surely come, the time to live – or the time to die . . .

552 09485 4 – 40p   T130

THE WILLING FLESH by WILLI HEINRICH

Sergeant Steiner was in command of ten men – survivors of a German rearguard trapped fifty miles behind the Russian lines. Their path to freedom led straight through the whole Russian army, together with all the murderous hazards of war – hunger, exhaustion, treachery, death. In the end, Steiner and his men were no longer fighting for Fuehrer or Fatherland, but for their naked, desperate lives . . .

The savage novel of the death throes of the German Wehrmacht.

552 09484 6 – 40p   T131

REIGN OF HELL by SVEN HASSEL

Burning, looting, raping, murdering, Hitler's Penal Regiments advanced on the centre of Warsaw leaving in their wake a bloody trail of death and destruction. They killed indiscriminately. Pole or German; young or old; man, woman, child – anyone who crossed their path was eliminated. For Himmler had sworn that Warsaw would be razed to the ground – if it took every member of the German army to do it! And against the Fuehrer's expendable battalions, for whom life had no meaning, the battle for Warsaw became an inferno – an endless reign of hell . . .

0 552 09178 2 – 60p   T114

YELLOW PERIL by GILBERT HACKFORTH-JONES
Noel Coward's lines – (with acknowledgements) –

> It's such a surprise when the British own the earth
> They give rise to such hilarity and mirth

– are the inspiration behind Gilbert Hackforth-Jones' nostalgic picture of naval life in North China in the latter part of the 1920's.

In that far-flung outpost of the Empire, on which at that period of history the sun never set, the naval warriors, on whose hands peacetime hung heavily, were busily occupying their minds and bodies in delight of simple things such as sport and womenfolk – until the menace of the Yellow Peril interceded in twenty-four hours of tragi-comedy.

0 552 09259 2 – 35p   T106

ONE OF THE FEW by Gp. Capt. J. A. KENT

He became the leader of one of the most successful fighter squadrons in World War II . . . Group Captain Johnny Kent – the man whose skilful leadership helped the famous 303 Squadron to play such a decisive part in the Battle of Britain, and won him the highest Polish military award, the *Virtuti Militari*.

This is Captain Kent's own story of his life in the R.A.F. – it is a story of triumphant achievement in combat and of a man whose air force career certainly picked him out as *One of the Few* . . .

'J. A. Kent's story is told modestly and without heroics, yet it gives a genuinely vivid impression of the way the work was done and many sound technical explanations.'

0 552 090692 X – 50p

T227

THE SHADOW WAR by HENRI MICHEL

They were an army without a flag – an army whose weapons were pitifully inadequate and whose training left much to be desired. But during the Second World War they caused chaos and disruption to many of the plans and strategies of the Third Reich . . .

'They' were the Resistance fighters – small bands of ordinary working people in Scandinavia, Holland, France, Greece and Poland who fought with everything they had towards the attainment of one single goal . . . victory over the Germans.

The Shadow War is the complete story of the brave men and women whose courage so often went unnoticed and whose operations were some of the closest-kept secrets of the war. . . .

0 552 09727 6 – 75p

T229

A SELECTED LIST OF WAR BOOKS
APPEARING IN CORGI

All these books are available at your bookshop or newsagent ; or can be ordered direct from the publisher. Just tick the titles you want and fill in the form below.

CORGI BOOKS, Cash Sales Department, P.O. Box 11, Falmouth, Cornwall.
Please send cheque or postal order, no currency.

U.K. and Eire send 15p for first book plus 5p per copy for each additional book ordered to a maximum charge of 50p to cover the cost of postage and packing.

Overseas Customers and B.F.P.O. allow 20p for first book and 10p per copy for each additional book.

NAME (Block letters) ....

ADDRESS ....

(SEPT 75)..

While every effort is made to keep prices low, it is sometimes necessary to increase prices at short notice. Corgi Books reserve the right to show new retail prices on covers which may differ from those previously advertised in the text or elsewhere.